FREEDOM WHEREVER WE GO

Freedom Wherever We Go

A BUDDHIST MONASTIC CODE
FOR THE 21ST CENTURY

Thich Nhat Hanh

PARALLAX PRESS
BERKELEY, CALIFORNIA

Parallax Press
P.O. Box 7355
Berkeley, California 94707
www.parallax.org

Parallax Press is the publishing division
of Unified Buddhist Church, Inc.

Cover and text design by Gopa & Ted 2, Inc.
Author photograph by Don Farber
This book is printed on 50% recycled paper. ♻

Library of Congress Cataloging-in-Publication Data

Nhât Hanh, Thích.
  Freedom wherever we go : a Buddhist monastic code
for the 21st century / Thich Nhat Hanh.
    p. cm.
  ISBN 1-888375-44-2 (pbk.)
  1. Monasticism and religious orders, Buddhist—Rules. 2.
Monastic and religious life (Buddhism) I. Title.

BQ6122.N53 2004
294.3'657—dc22
                                    2004012986

1 2 3 4 5 6 7 / 10 09 08 07 06 05 04

Table of Contents

Preface

THE PRATIMOKSHA is the basic book of training for Buddhist monastics. Training with the Pratimoksha, monastics purify their bodies and minds, cultivate love for all beings, and advance on the path of liberation. "Prati" means step-by-step. It can also be translated as "going in a direction." "Moksha" means liberation. So "Pratimoksha" can be translated as freedom at every step. Each precept brings freedom to a specific area of our daily life. If we keep the precept of not drinking alcohol, for example, we have the freedom of not being drunk. If we keep the precept of not stealing, we have the freedom of not being in prison. The word "Pratimoksha" can also mean "in every place there is liberation." We have titled this revised version of the Pratimoksha *Freedom Wherever We Go* to remind us that we are going in the direction of liberation.

As a part of their training at Plum Village, fully ordained monks and nuns must spend at least five years studying the *Vinaya*, a vast and rich body of literature, that defines and organizes the life of the monastic community. This study of the Vinaya includes the Revised and the Classical Pratimoksha. Monastics study the Vinaya not as professors or specialists, but as practitioners. They study with a clear insight that the trainings, mindful manners, and regulations are the foundation for the survival of the Sangha. The renewed and updated version of the Pratimoksha can inspire the monastic Sangha of today to rediscover the integrity, simplicity, beauty, and freedom of monastic life.

During the fifth year of his ministry, the Buddha and his senior disciples began to create the Pratimoksha for the monastic community. The precepts were established over several decades, each responding to the needs and situations of the Original Sangha of the Buddha. When the Buddha was about to enter Nirvana, he told his attendant, the Venerable Ananda, that the minor and lesser rules could be removed, so that the text would remain light, relevant, and appropriate. At that time, Ananda did not inquire which specific trainings the Buddha was referring to. So after the Buddha's passing into Nirvana, the elder monk Kassyapa did not dare to remove any of the precepts. Two thousand six hundred years have gone by, and this recommendation by the Buddha has not been carried out.

Two hundred years after the Buddha's passing, some twenty schools of Buddhism arose, each with its own Vinaya. The Vinayas which are found in various schools of Buddhism all have their roots in the Buddha's original teachings and practice. The Pratimoksha is the heart of the Vinaya. It is a text that fully ordained monks and nuns recite twice a month in the Uposatha ceremony to nourish and maintain the purity of their vows. In Vietnam and China, most monks and nuns recite the Pratimoksha of the Dharmagupta school of Buddhism. In Sri Lanka, Thailand, and Burma the monks recite the Pratimoksha that belongs to the Tamrasatiya (Theravada) school. The Dharmagupta Pratimoksha for monks has 250 precepts, and the Tamrasatiya Pratimoksha for monks has 227 precepts. Except for some small differences, the texts of these two major traditions are nearly identical to one another.

Buddhism should remain a living tradition. Like a tree, the dead branches need to be pruned in order for new shoots to grow. The new shoots are the teachings and practices that respond to the needs of our present time and culture. Technological developments, mass media, and the speed of modern life have all influenced the life of monastic communities. Degradation of the monastic lifestyle is evident in places all over the world, in both Buddhist and non-Buddhist communities. To respond to this present situation, a revised Pratimoksha is urgently needed.

In our effort to make the Revised Pratimoksha as relevant and responsive as possible, the Dharma Teacher Council of Plum Village has consulted extensively with Vinaya teachers and other monks and nuns in Vietnam and elsewhere over the past five years. In addition, we have drawn upon our experience of monastic life in the West over the past two decades. Therefore, the Revised Pratimoksha aims to offer guidance and support to contemporary Buddhist monastics living both in Asia and in the West.

The Revised Pratimoksha was first released on March 31, 2003 at the Choong Ang Sangha University in Seoul, Korea—one of the Mahayana Buddhist countries of Asia. In the Revised Pratimoksha, we have substituted trainings that are no longer appropriate to our time with new trainings that are essential to protect the practice and integrity of monastic members. For example, in the classical version of the Pratimoksha there is a precept that advises the monastics to travel only by foot. The precept reads: "If a bhikshuni who is not ill rides in a vehicle, she offends against the Payantika precepts." This rule was appropriate for the time and place of the Buddha, when traveling by vehicle was unusual and generally a mark of high status and wealth. But coming to the U.S.A. in the 21st century, for instance, if the Buddha tried to walk on the highway instead of riding in a car, he might get hurt or arrested. To respond to the needs of modern monastics the Revised Pratimoksha has trainings that address the use of cars, computers, television, mobile telephones, electronic games, e-mail, and the Internet.

There have been people who have asked us: "Who are you to change the monastic codes made by the Buddha?" Our answer is always: "We are the children of the Buddha. We are his continuation, and we are practicing to carry out his wishes." The Buddha invested much of his time and energy to teach and train monks and nuns. Buddhism has survived to this day because monastic Sanghas have been continuously maintained. The purpose of the Revised Pratimoksha is to protect the freedom and integrity of monastic practice, so that the authentic path of liberation can continue.

For Buddhism to remain a living tradition, the teaching and practice should remain relevant. The Pratimoksha should not be merely an object of academic or intellectual study. There are already many Vinaya masters who are well-versed in the Vinaya literature and capable of teaching and explaining it eloquently. The main purpose of the Pratimoksha is to offer concrete guidance to fully ordained monks and nuns. We are certain that the Buddha counts on the insight, intelligence, and courage of his descendants to continue making the path of liberation accessible and open to our current generation. Therefore, revising the teaching and the practice is truly necessary.

This is the first time our tradition has made this text available to lay readers. We believe that making this text available will nourish the practice and strength of the Fourfold Sangha of monks, nuns, laymen, and laywomen. Reading the Pratimoksha allows lay practitioners to understand the monastic codes of conduct as well as the monastic lifestyle.

Reading the Pratimoksha also inspires us to live our daily lives with compassion, love, and understanding so that we can protect and care for ourselves, our loved ones, the environment, and all living beings.

We have revised the Pratimoksha to pay tribute to our root teacher, Shakyamuni Buddha, and all our ancestral teachers, who have transmitted the wonderful Dharma to our current generation. We trust that only by keeping Buddhism truly alive and free from degradation and corruption can we be authentic descendants of the Buddha.

—Thich Nhat Hanh and the
Dharma Teacher Council of Plum Village

FREEDOM WHEREVER WE GO

Introduction: Precepts Are Mindfulness

WHEN I WAS A YOUNG MONK, I learned that the three essential trainings of a practitioner are precepts, concentration, and insight. In the Vinaya, the collection of rules and regulations for monastics, it is taught that the precepts lead to concentration, concentration leads to insight, and insight leads you to realize the path. Although I learned this, I could not really accept what the elder monks taught me. I obeyed them, I listened to what they said, but I did not feel satisfied with what they were telling me. In my head I still had the question: how can precepts lead to concentration? Perhaps because I understood the word "precepts" as meaning "don't do this, don't do that." It is good not to drink alcohol, not to tell lies, and not to kill. But how can these things give birth to concentration? That question lay in my head as a young novice. Fortunately, ten years later, I was able to understand.

I had been told that before the Buddha passed into Nirvana he said, "Please look at the Vinaya as your teacher." I did not dare oppose this. I did not dare say, "How is this possible?" But I did not really believe it. I saw the precepts as preventing us from doing something wrong and I thought, how could the Buddha just be someone who prevents us from doing things?

One day, I recognized that, in the teachings of the Noble Eightfold Path and the teachings of the Five Powers, concentration and insight are always preceded by mindfulness. The Five Powers are faith, diligence, mindfulness, concentration, and insight. Faith has an energy which leads to diligence and diligence leads to the power of mindfulness. The power of mindfulness leads to the power of concentration which in turn leads to the power of insight.

It is very reasonable that mindfulness can lead to concentration. When our mind is attentive to something, it is not dispersed in something else. When we are drinking tea, our mind is wholly in the act of drinking tea. I am drinking tea and I know I am drinking tea. Mindfulness very naturally leads to concentration. Actually, the energy of mindfulness already contains the energy of concentration. We could say that mindfulness contains concentration and concentration contains insight.

In the Noble Eightfold Path, Right Mindfulness precedes Right Concentration. Right Concentration precedes Right View. Right View is insight. In the basic teachings of the Buddha, we always have mindfulness followed by concentration and insight. At the same time, the Vinaya teaches us the three basic trainings of precepts, concentration, and insight. From precepts comes concentration, from concentration comes insight. Comparing the Vinaya with the Noble Eightfold Path, I discovered that precepts are mindfulness. This was a very important discovery in my life. The ancestral teachers and my own teachers had not taught me this directly; maybe they realized it but they had not actually said it. *If the basis of precepts is not mindfulness, they are not authentic precepts.*

Mindful of the suffering caused by killing, we make a strong determination to refrain from killing. We are mindful of the suffering that we ourselves will experience if we kill and we are mindful of the suffering other living beings will experience if we kill. Our mindfulness shows us clearly the path of emancipation. Without mindfulness, how could we be aware of suffering, the causes of suffering, and the path leading to the cessation of suffering? That is why we have called the five precepts for laypeople and the fourteen precepts of the Community of Interbeing "mindfulness trainings." Practicing the precepts, we train ourselves in mindfulness. With mindfulness we can easily touch the essence of each precept.

As I learned as a novice, we cannot only accept someone else's experience and insight regarding the practice of the precepts. We must taste it for ourselves. We must have our own experience of the precepts to fully understand their essence.

Practicing the Substance of the Precepts

The Buddha taught that we have a tendency to get caught in five kinds of wrong views. The first wrong view is thinking that you are only your body. The second wrong view is being caught in an extreme or dualistic view. The third wrong view is being caught in a misperception, a distorted view, or an upside-down view. The fourth wrong view is being stuck in a particular point of view or doctrine, which prevents you from going any further in your insight or understanding. The fifth kind of wrong view is being caught in the outer form of rites and rituals. We think that if we avoid doing what is forbidden and follow all rules and regulations, we will be liberated. We are content to follow rules and perform rituals without understanding their significance.

There are spiritual traditions based on forbidding certain things and performing certain rites and rituals. The followers of these traditions believe that, thanks to these rites and rituals and these prohibitive rules, they will become enlightened. But in fact, often they become slaves to these rites and regulations and never attain freedom. When we are caught in rituals, we can also be caught in the various rules and regulations which are attached to these rites and rituals. When studying the precepts and putting them into practice we need to be careful not to fall into the fifth kind of wrong view, by being caught in the outer form of practicing the precepts.

We tend to get caught in superstitious beliefs that do not bring us understanding and transformation. We may believe we cannot put the Buddha statue near the place where we urinate. Or that if we give someone a present, we cannot give them a knife because it will break our relationship. Or we believe that if we live on the thirteenth floor it will bring us bad luck. In the time of the Buddha, the Hindu religion emphasized rites and rituals. Often people did not practice or understand the real spirit of these rituals, but practiced them just as an empty form. In response, the Buddha cautioned us against the wrong view of being caught in the outer form of rites and rituals.

We still have this tendency. We are caught in the outer form of the practice. We chant a sutra but actually our mind is somewhere else; we are not in contact with the meaning of the sutra. We do not gain any insight.

If we keep the precepts but are caught in their outer form and do not understand their deeper meaning, our practice cannot lead to liberation, purity, peace, and joy. For example, we may think that the more we invoke the Buddha's name, the more holy and pure we will become. Yet if we invoke the Buddha's name without mindfulness and concentration, it will not bring us any benefit. We can repeat the Buddha's name thousands of times a day but if we are still carried away by our irritation or unhappiness while we practice then we are caught in the outer form. Or suppose we eat a vegetarian diet but we do not enjoy it. It makes us suffer and we always think of how nice it would be to eat meat. This is being caught in the form. We do not touch the essence of the practice of protecting life, of not harming living beings. When we practice the content, the essence of the precepts, we receive the benefit of peace, clarity, and freedom right away.

The basis of meaningful rules or regulations must be mindfulness, wisdom, and understanding. The reason I do not eat the flesh of living beings is because I do not want to harm my heart of compassion. I am not vegetarian because I believe it will bring me a lot of merit in the future. If I am practicing the substance of the precepts, when I eat a vegetarian meal, I feel happy and peaceful. I don't even realize that I am eating a vegetarian meal. I just feel content; I don't suffer at all. I simply enjoy that I am not eating the flesh of living beings. This happiness is based on mindfulness. I am mindful that when I eat meat, other beings must suffer and I myself suffer. Mindfulness is the real spirit of the precepts.

As a young novice nun, if our elder sister tells us that according to the precepts we have to stop listening to romantic music, we may suffer because we may be caught in this kind of music. When the young novice listens to this kind of music, it may make her feel joyful and when she is forced to stop, she suffers. If she feels this way, she is caught in the wrong view of rules and regulations. On the other hand, if she understands that listening to romantic music will water the seeds of romantic love in her and she doesn't want these seeds to be watered, she can easily give it up without being angry. She is aware that listening to sentimental music has an unwholesome influence on her practice as a monastic and therefore she is very happy to be able to let go of it. That is mindfulness. That is practicing the substance of the precept, and not being caught in the outer form of regulations.

There is a very old sutra called the Paramattha Sutta, the Sutra on the Highest Truth. It is found in a collection of sutras called the Sutta Nipata which scholars believe to be the oldest teachings given by the Buddha. These sutras were learned by heart by the monks and nuns in the time of the Buddha. The Buddha taught these sutras before the Sangha had any monastery to live in—they were just walking from place to place without any settled home.

In the Sutra on the Highest Truth, the Buddha says clearly that when we believe that the outer form of ceremonies, rites, and rituals are the only means to achieve awakening and liberation, we are caught. The sutra says that to go towards enlightenment we should not be caught in our knowledge of the teachings, we should not be caught in regulations, or in the outer form of ceremonies.

Keeping the precepts because we feel pressured or forced to do so, or in order to gain merit in the future stems from our wrong views of the precepts. Rather, we should keep the precepts with the aim of understanding our suffering and finding skillful means to end suffering. Instead of saying, "Do not kill," we say, "Aware that killing brings about suffering in my society, I shall not kill, I shall protect life." This precept is mindfulness. If we want to have happiness and liberation, we have to keep the precepts as a practice of mindfulness. True, authentic precepts are based on Right Mindfulness. My great discovery as a young monk was that the precepts are not taboos; they are not something taking away your freedom. Precepts are Right Mindfulness. Practicing the precepts in the spirit of Right Mindfulness will lead to Right Concentration which will lead to deep understanding.

The Sutra on the Fruits of the Monastic Path

The Samanaphala Sutta is the sutra given to King Ajatasattu. It means "The fruits of the monk's practice." "Samana" means "monk," "phala" means "fruit." If you read the Samanaphala Sutta you will understand the meaning of the Pratimoksha. Ajatasattu killed his own father to become the king. After this he felt so much guilt that he became mentally ill. The king went to many different spiritual leaders for advice, but he was not satisfied and his mental illness worsened. Then the doctor Jivaka advised him to see the Buddha, convinced that only the Buddha could cure his mental illness. The king agreed to go and asked Doctor Jivaka to accompany him. The doctor said, "When we visit the Buddha tonight you will see that he is surrounded by hundreds of monks in the meditation hall."

It was nighttime when the king, queen, and their followers arrived. It was very quiet, because the monks made no noise. The king was afraid that it was a trap and that he would be killed, because he had caused troubles to the Buddha in the past. He had helped Devadatta, the Buddha's cousin, form a new congregation, trying to make Devadatta a new Buddha. He had also supported a plot to murder the Buddha. So he asked, "Are they waiting there to ambush me?" The doctor replied, "Your majesty, don't say that. Look through the door. The Buddha and all his disciples are sitting there in peace." He opened the door and saw a thousand monks sitting in complete silence. He had never seen a thousand people sitting together in silence. The king was moved and was no longer fearful.

The Buddha offered the king a seat and invited him to ask a question. The king asked, "I want to know what the benefits of becoming a monk or a nun are. I see a thousand people with their heads shaved, wearing the monk's robe, living the simple life, having left behind their family, their wealth, and the honors of the world. Thousands of people are going on this path. What is the benefit for them?" The Buddha asked, "Your majesty, have you ever asked this question before?" King Ajatasattu answered, "I have. I have asked other spiritual leaders but I have never heard a satisfactory answer." The Buddha then delivered the Samana-phala Sutta.

The Buddha said, "Great king, say there is a slave working from dawn until late at night to serve his master, year after year. One day he thinks, my master is a human being; I am also a human being. Why is he free and I a slave? Why do I have to work hard from morning till night? Why don't I leave this life behind and find freedom? Thinking like that, he runs away from his master. He goes to a spiritual teacher and asks to become a monk, to practice mindful walking, eating one meal a day, and wearing the patchwork robe. He feels so free, so at ease, so happy. Your majesty, if you saw someone like that would you tell him, 'You have to come and work for me from morning till night. You have to do this, you have to do that.' Would you force him to do that?" The king said, "No, I wouldn't. He is a monk. I have no right to make him a slave again, to make him work from morning to night, doing this and that. I would give him a robe, food, shelter and medicine."

The Buddha said, "Great king, he may have only been a monk for two months and he is already released from so much bondage. He is no longer discriminated against. There is no longer any racial discrimination, social discrimination, or slavery when you become a monk. This is one of the fruits of being a monk. When you become a Buddhist monk you no longer belong to a caste, whether it is untouchable or brahmin."

The king said, "Oh, wonderful, tell us more."

"This monk practices 250 precepts and every one of them leads to freedom. Because of not drinking alcohol, that person is free from being drunk. Because of not stealing, he is free from the fear of being arrested. Thanks to the practice of the precepts, you can guarantee your freedom and you do not fall into bondage. You will not be arrested by the police. When you become a monk you only have three robes and a bowl, so you don't have to be afraid of anything. No one will rob you. You sit at the foot of a tree in freedom, in joy, in peace, without any fear, anxiety, or craving. This is the second fruit of practicing as a monk or a nun."

The king said, "Oh wonderful, World Honored One, please tell us more." The Buddha said, "As a monk we don't have to worry about eating, we only eat once a day. We consume little so that we have plenty of time to enjoy our life, to watch the sky, to look at the mountains." The Buddha said, "When we become a monk we have time to practice liberation. We do walking meditation, we enjoy mindful breathing, we cultivate joy and happiness everyday. Out in the world people worry and grieve. Monks have a lot of time to nourish happiness and joy. This is the third fruit of the monks' life."

"Oh wonderful, World Honored One, tell us more." The Buddha continued, "When we have happiness and joy, our path to liberation is very easy. We can look deeply and see that everything is interdependent; we do not have a separate self. We are able to touch our nature of no-birth, no-death, no-coming, and no-going. We have liberation; we are completely secure. There is nothing higher than this liberation." "How wonderful, World Honored One." "The next thing is that you can help many people when you are liberated, you can help them not to suffer; that is a great fruit." The king said, "Wonderful, World Honored Lord. I have never heard such wonderful teachings as these. Hearing such teachings

I have faith in the path of liberation; I have found a path to put an end to all my wrongdoing." From then on his mental illness improved day by day.

The message of The Sutra on the Fruits of the Monastic Path is that happiness is made of liberation. The basis of the precepts is freedom. The word "precepts" as it is used here does not mean something that binds us or takes away our freedom. It is the opposite—precepts guarantee our freedom and our happiness. When we practice the precepts freely and happily, we are practicing the precepts in a true and authentic way.

This story is similar to the story of Baddhiya. He belonged to the royal family of the Sakya clan. He had been a provincial governor and became a monk with Ananda and Upali. One night in sitting meditation, Baddhiya experienced so much happiness that he could not bear it and he said, "Oh my happiness, oh my happiness, oh my happiness!" There was a monk sitting near Baddhiya who heard him and misunderstood. He thought that Baddhiya was longing for all the happiness he'd had in the past, when he was a powerful man, of a noble, wealthy family. So this monk told the Buddha about Baddhiya.

The Buddha knew his disciples, but all the same he called Baddhiya to him and in the presence of many other monks he asked, "Baddhiya, is it true that last night when you were doing sitting meditation you cried out three times 'oh my happiness'?" Baddhiya said, "Yes I did." The Buddha asked Baddhiya to explain. He said, "In the past when I was a governor, I had great wealth and many bodyguards around me but I was so afraid. I was afraid people would steal everything I had, or kill me. I was overwhelmed by fear day and night. Now all I have is three robes and a bowl and I sit at the foot of a tree and feel so much freedom. I cannot bear it. My happiness is so great! That is why I had to shout out 'Oh my happiness!' If I disturbed other monks who were meditating I express my regret, I am very sorry." The happiness of a monk or a nun is that we are not afraid of losing anything because we have nothing to lose.

The Precepts Were Created in Community

In Christianity and in Judaism, commandments are believed to have been revealed by God. On Mount Sinai, God gave Moses the Ten Commandments, engraved on stone by fire. Moses brought the commandments down to his society for the people to practice. In Buddhism, the Buddha is not considered a god or a lawmaker; he did not have a blueprint of the precepts. Instead, the precepts evolved in relation to the needs and aspirations of the dynamic and living community that surrounded the Buddha.

One time the Venerable Shariputra asked the Lord Buddha, "Why don't you create precepts?" The Buddha said, "I do not need to create precepts. We make a precept only when something goes wrong, to help people avoid falling into that harmful situation again." We know that the Buddha was not a lawmaker. The Buddha only devised a precept when there was a need. Once it was devised, if it was not perfect in that form, it could be corrected or abandoned in favor of a different precept. This is a wonderful attitude to have. If we are caught in the outer form of the precepts and say that they cannot be changed because changing them is disrespectful to the Buddha, we are going in the opposite direction of what the Buddha wants. We have to keep correcting and making the precepts more beautiful if we want to be loyal to the idea and the spirit of the Buddha.

The Buddha did not devise the precepts on his own. He always worked in consultation with his lay and monastic disciples. He also learned from other spiritual communities, like the Jain Order under Mahavira. There were things that the Buddha saw were helpful for the practice, and therefore he put them into the Buddhist precepts. Before the time of the Buddha, the Brahmins had a great deal power. At times they misused their spiritual influence and caused damage to society. In response to the Brahmins corruption and abuse of power, there was a movement called the Shramana movement. The Buddhist and Jain Orders were two schools that were part of this Shramana movement. When Jains went on almsround they put out their bowls to receive food. They did not take the food directly with their hands. This is how they practiced humility and non-greed in receiving offerings. This way of going on almsround was also adopted in the Buddhist precepts.

In addition, the precept which prohibits nuns from bathing naked came from the advice of a laywoman, the mother of Migara. She lived in Rajagriha and offered a beautiful monastery to the Buddha. One day she saw the nuns bathing naked and told the Buddha. So the Buddha made a precept about this. The precept that prohibits children from being ordained without their parents' permission comes from the Buddha's father, King Suddhodana. Many of the precepts come from the lay and monastic disciples of the Buddha who saw what was needed to help the Sangha.

The Middle Way

It is clear that the Buddha wanted us to practice the precepts in a natural way, without being too austere or too relaxed. The cousin of the Buddha, Devadatta, at one time tried to cause a split in the Buddha's Sangha by setting up a new community and attracting many members of the Sangha to follow him. He claimed that the Buddha was too lenient in his practice and teaching of the precepts. He created a series of new precepts and said that these would lead the monks to a superior practice. These precepts included rules like: monks could only sleep under trees and could not take shelter in huts; monks could only use discarded cloth for making their robes and could not use new cloth; monks could only receive alms and could not accept invitations to eat in laypeople's homes. The Buddha did not forbid the monks from doing any of these things, but looking deeply he saw that if these regulations were enforced for the whole Sangha, not everyone could practice them. Therefore, he did not agree to adopt these as precepts. He saw that they were too austere and would limit the number of people who could successfully practice the monastic path.

There were also monks who took the precepts too lightly, saying, "I have attained so much realization on the path, I no longer need to observe these precepts." Or they would say, "These are minor details that do not truly relate to the path of liberation, so why should I practice all these things?" Staying flexible and appropriate to the situation, we find the dynamic balance which we can call the Middle Way.

The Buddha was aware that the precepts might bring more controversy and dissension in the Sangha even after his passing away. He predicted that there would not be dissension concerning his essential teachings but that there would be dissension concerning the practice of the Vinaya. Shortly after the Buddha's passing, 500 monks gathered to recall and collect all the teachings of the Buddha. Several hundred years later, the second major council was called with 700 monks. This second council was assembled to resolve an issue concerning transgressions of minor precepts referred to as the "ten transgressions."

When the Buddha was with his Sangha near Kosambi, there was a serious dispute in the Sangha that arose from a minor transgression of the precepts. A Dharma Teacher had not properly cared for and put away a washing basin which he had used. The Vinaya Master accused him of transgressing this minor precept. The Dharma Teacher was not able to accept the accusation and protested. The disciples of the Dharma Teacher heard of the accusation and also protested. As a result, the Sangha was nearly split in half. Some of the laypeople, hearing of the disagreement, also chose sides, making offerings to monks on only one side of the dispute.

When the Buddha learned of the situation he invited the bell to gather together the entire Sangha of monks in Kosambi. He advised the monks to let go of their dissension and make peace. The monks did not listen and the situation persisted. A second time the Buddha assembled the monks and requested that they release their resentment and restore harmony in their community. This time the monks retorted that the Buddha was advanced in age, and should not bother them but leave them alone to deal with their own situation. The Buddha was disheartened by this response and withdrew to the forest for some time.

What the Buddha cared about most was the harmony and happiness of the Sangha. What made him most unhappy was division in the Sangha. Some time later the monks had the opportunity to begin anew with the Buddha and to reconcile themselves.

We should be aware of the tendency to provoke controversy and dissension in the Sangha with regard to the precepts. The precepts are guiding means; they are concrete expressions of the teachings to help us walk firmly and smoothly on the path of liberation, joy, and peace. We should study them not to accumulate knowledge or to dispute with others, but to strengthen the beauty, happiness, and freedom of the Sangha body.

Precepts Should Respond to the Situation

The Buddha said, "Although I have given you precepts for this particular time and place, if you come to a certain place and the laws of that land are different, you should not use the precepts that have been given to you here. You should not practice in a way that goes against the laws of the land where you are living." The Buddha also said, "There may be precepts I have not yet devised, but if you come to a part of the world where they are needed then you have to devise these precepts." In the classical Pratimoksha there is no precept about not taking drugs, for example. Buddha did not formulate a precept forbidding us from using and selling drugs because in those times they did not have drugs to use and to sell. However, in modern times perhaps it needs to be stated that to maintain their freedom and clarity, it is advisable that monks and nuns should not use and sell drugs. Therefore, it makes sense to have a precept about this in the Revised Pratimoksha.

In the Mahaprajnaparamita Shastra, our ancestral teacher Nagarjuna says that the precepts the Buddha devised for us have to be looked on as appropriate truth; they are not absolute. There are precepts which are formulated specifically to deal with special situations. We can say that they are a means to an end. If there is no special situation, this precept does not need to be used. For example, some of the precepts in the Revised Pratimoksha say that a monk or nun cannot receive payment from the government or be an employee of the government. As monastics, we cannot be a spy of the government. We cannot work for a political party or receive payment from a political party. In the U.S. and France we don't really need this precept. It is only in Vietnam that monks and nuns are sometimes paid by the government. This particular precept is needed in Vietnam to deal with the situation there. In the future, if no one is paid by the government and these precepts are no longer applicable, they can be removed.

Precepts are intended to deal with real situations we face. Above all there is the society around us and the precepts have to be appropriate to this situation. For example, in Vietnam we use the lunar calendar, so the day for reciting the precepts was chosen according to this calendar. But in the West, we use the solar calendar, so rather than reciting the precepts on the fifteenth and the thirtieth day of the lunar month, we recite the precepts every other Tuesday or some other day of the week. That is to practice in accord with our society.

The Nuns' Precepts

Each precept was devised in response to a particular situation and for the benefit that the precept would bring. For instance, in order to allow women to become nuns, eight special precepts were created. At first the Buddha refused to allow his stepmother, Gotami, and other women to become nuns because the Buddha felt that his society would not accept this. Then the Venerable Ananda came to the Buddha and shared about the gratitude the Buddha owed to Gotami, and encouraged the Buddha to allow her to ordain. After refusing twice, the Buddha finally accepted. He discussed the matter with the elder monks and they found a way to open the door of the Sangha and allow women to become nuns. That door was the eight Garudharmas, the eight precepts of respect. These were not absolute truths by any means, rather they were just a door to allow Gotami and women after her to enter the Sangha.

In revising the Pratimoksha, we have kept the traditional number of trainings for monks and nuns. There are still 250 trainings for monks, and 348 for nuns. In the Buddha's time admitting women to the ordained community was a revolution. In order to allow women to become nuns, they were asked to follow certain guidelines to maintain the customary relations between men and women of that time, such as showing respect to all monks regardless of ordination age, not criticizing monks, and requesting teachings and guidance from monks. In addition, the nuns received all of the precepts for monks (except for a few that are not relevant for women) as well as additional precepts created for the nuns. After the Buddha passed away, the nuns also created more precepts for themselves. For this reason, in the Classical Pratimoksha, there were more precepts for nuns than for monks.

The Revised Pratimoksha for bhikshunis has been created with the guidance and support of many senior nuns in Vietnam and it was their request to maintain the traditional number of precepts for nuns, so as to respond adequately to the needs of the nuns' community. It will be up to current and future generations of bhikshus and bhikshunis to continue to make the monks' and nuns' precepts a true reflection of their needs and aspirations.

In the process of revising the Pratimoksha we may also look deeply into these numbers. We do not have to stick with the classical number of precepts. We know that the number of precepts was continuously changing during the lifetime of the Buddha and in the period after the Buddha. As we continue to revise and refine the Pratimoksha we may take into consideration the Buddha's recommendation, not being caught in the exact number of precepts.

Keeping the Precepts Alive and Flexible

Some precepts had to be revised seven or eight times depending on the situation. They were living and flexible. For example, the precept about keeping food overnight was formed in response to a certain situation and it was changed a number of times. In the time of the Buddha, in principle a bhikshu did not have the right to keep food overnight. But there were some monks who had to go on a long journey crossing a desert. They traveled for many days where there were no villages where they could beg for food. So they were given permission to take some dried food with them. Therefore, the precept of not keeping food overnight can only be applied in the case in which we can stay in one place and beg for alms each day.

Once, during a time of hunger, the laypeople wished to offer food to the monks so that the monks could stay alive. The laypeople could not be present to offer food every day so they asked the monks to keep enough food to last them for a number of days. If the monks had not received the food, some of them might have died of hunger. At that time the Buddha allowed them to keep food, but only outside the monastery. The food had to be dried. Some monks were in charge of drying the food. Every day they would put it in the sun to be dried. The difficulty was that the crows came and ate some of the food and other hungry people also took some. Consequentially, the monks did not have enough to eat. So the Buddha said, "Okay, you can dry the food inside the monastery." That was a compromise; that was flexibility. In principle monks could not keep food overnight or cook food in the monastery. But in a time of hunger if the Sangha had been rigid about this, monks and nuns would have died.

There was another time in Kosambi when the monks had nothing to eat. The Venerable Shariputra saw that the grass was growing well so he surmised that there must be some nutrition in the earth. He said, "Let us turn the grass over, take the earth and soak it in water and maybe the nutritive elements will come out of the earth. We can drink it and perhaps it will help us to stay alive." At that time a horse owner passed by who had some bran which he fed to his horses. He saw that the monks were so thin. He said, "Monks, if you like, you can pass by my stables every day and I will give you some of the bran which I give the horses to eat." The Buddha was also given a fistful of bran each day. Ananda felt sorry for the Buddha and wanted to roast the bran a bit so it would taste better for the Buddha. The Buddha refused because, according to the precepts, monks could not cook in the monastery. He would not allow Ananda to do it. But later, he allowed monks to keep food overnight and also to cook food in special circumstances.

There is a precept in the Classical Pratimoksha prohibiting monks from receiving money, gold, or silver. Once, Migara's mother gave an offering, a bag with some silver money. None of the monks dared to receive it. Then they discussed the matter with the Buddha and found that they could resolve the difficulty in this way: they could give the money to a layperson and when they needed something essential, such as medicine or food, they could ask that layperson to provide it for them. They called this layperson the "pure person." If monastics were offered money, they did not have the right to receive it. But if there was a pure person there, they could give it to that person and when they needed something this person could buy it for them. In this way they did not break the precepts. Things like this happened in the community of the Buddha. The Buddha and his disciples were able to resolve difficult situations by revising the precepts.

Another example of the Buddha's flexibility is with regard to the age requirement for ordination. Originally, the Buddha said that anyone wishing to ordain had to be twenty years old. But when his son Rahula wanted to become a monk the Buddha brought the age requirement down to fifteen. Then one day the Vinaya Master Upali ordained seventeen children under the age of twelve, to save them from dying of hunger. The children were not used to eating only one meal a day, so they cried at night. The Buddha heard them and asked where they came from. When the monks explained what happened, the Buddha responded that children must be twelve years old before the Sangha can allow them into the monastery, so that they would be old enough to eat only one meal a day. Even today, sometimes the nuns in Vietnam allow children to live in the temple in order to have something to eat and they can become monks and nuns later on if they want to.

There is a precept stating that in order to conduct a monastic ordination, there must be ten monks present as officiators and witnesses. But in the time of the Buddha, there were very few monks in the frontier areas. If they had to wait for ten monks to arrive on foot or by ox cart, it would take very long. So the Buddha gave permission for these areas to have only five monks present for the ordination. The Buddha was very kind, very flexible. Similarly, in these frontier areas, it was very painful to walk on the earth because it was covered with sharp stones. For this reason the Buddha allowed the monks in these areas to wear shoes made with three layers of soles, so they wouldn't get sore feet, instead of the customary single sole. In another area where it rained a lot, the Buddha allowed the monks to sit on animal skins, which was otherwise forbidden. The precepts are made to help people not to suffer. When the Buddha was so flexible, why should we be so rigid about the precepts?

The Day for Purifying Our Precepts' Body

In the time of the Buddha, the Uposatha day for reciting the precepts was a very joyful occasion for the monks and nuns. The monks had the opportunity to be together all day as did the nuns. In the first months after the Buddha began teaching, there were no precepts. But in Hindu communities, they had precepts and came together every two weeks to recite them. Their communities were older than the Buddha's Sangha. King Bimbisara came to the Buddha and said, "Why don't we also have a day twice a month for the monks to come together and enjoy each other as they do in other communities?"

Uposatha means "to nourish purity." The Uposatha day is to nourish our peace, and increase our purity and joy. When we keep the precepts it makes us light and pure. Then we can be happy. We have to have some purity already in order for it to grow. This purity is our precepts' body. Every one of us who has received some of the precepts has a precepts' body. When we receive the Five Mindfulness Trainings, we have that precepts' body. The reason we can be called a novice is because we have the ten precepts' body. When we receive the full precepts we have the Pratimoksha precepts' body. The way we nourish this body is by attending the Uposatha day and reciting the precepts. The observation and practice of the precepts makes our tree of purity grow.

If a monk or nun is unwell, he or she must ask to be represented and send their wishes to be there, saying that they are pure in keeping the precepts. We can call this "entrusting your aspiration." It is your aspiration to keep and nourish your precepts' body, it is your aspiration to be present for the recitation, but because you are sick you cannot attend.

The ceremony of reciting the precepts is an expedient means and it is an opportunity. If our precepts' body is not pure, we cannot recite the precepts. Therefore, if we want to recite the precepts, we have to make our precepts' body pure. We have to clean it, sweep it, and purify it before the Uposatha ceremony. That is why we have to practice the Beginning Anew ceremony before the precepts recitation. We cannot wait until the time for reciting the precepts to begin anew for any transgressions that we have made. We must do that before the recitation.

When everyone has entered the meditation hall for the recitation, we light incense and ask the question: "Is everyone's precepts' body pure?" We know everyone will say yes because everyone has prepared themselves before the ceremony. If we are not pure we cannot enter to recite the precepts. Knowing that the recitation day is about to arrive, the monks and nuns feel inspired to begin anew, to clear their offenses. Therefore the aim of reciting the precepts is to make everyone clean and pure again.

The Five-Part Vinaya states that if someone in the community has not kept the precepts, the recitation must be postponed. This is not to punish the person. Rather it encourages the whole community to support the offending member to retain his or her purity by admitting the offense, asking for the support and help of the community, and beginning anew. Aware that each member of the Sangha is a part of the Sangha body, when one person has made a mistake, the whole community is also responsible in some way. This is why we have to wait to recite the precepts until everyone's precepts' body is pure.

How do we re-establish purity? Purity is regained because we have practiced beginning anew, because we have observed the precepts. The object of the practice is to keep our precepts' body pure, not allowing it to be wounded, cracked, or broken. This is the responsibility of the whole community. We have to help each other to keep our precepts' body pure. Then the Uposatha day can be a happy day. There are many methods in the tradition which help us purify ourselves. We can learn about these methods and change those that need to be made more up to date. We don't just study the Vinaya in order to accumulate knowledge. We study so that we can make the Vinaya appropriate to our times and use it to purify our modern day precepts' body. In the past we did not wash our clothes with soap. We used ashes, herbs and such. Now we have detergents that clean our clothes more effectively. It is the same with the Vinaya. There should be new ways of cleaning our precepts' body.

Two Aims of the Precepts: Protecting the Sangha and Protecting the Individual

The first aim of the precepts is to preserve the reputation and the integrity of the Sangha. If the Sangha loses its reputation and is not respected, it will be destroyed and people will not have the opportunity to practice as monks and nuns.

There is a precept which states that when you go to a layperson's house you should not act in a disorderly way. In the Classical Pratimoksha, there are many precepts aimed at preserving the respect that people have for the Sangha. In the history of Plum Village, we have occasionally had to take action in accordance with the precepts to preserve the good reputation of the Sangha. We have had to send a few monks and nuns home when they have broken the most serious offenses in the Pratimoksha. All the bhikshus and bhikshunis had to meet to look deeply into the particular situation. Then, we asked these monks and nuns to return to lay life. We did this with the spirit of understanding and compassion, not to punish them. We held a tea meditation to say good-bye and we bought them a plane ticket home. These kinds of actions have always been taken in the past to protect the Sangha, so that people could continue to feel secure and at ease practicing with the Sangha. We also sent these monks and nuns home for their own protection. If they had remained monks and nuns, they may have caused a great deal of damage to themselves and to the Sangha. This would have been a big misfortune for them.

In fact, ninety percent of the difficulties in a community of practice can be resolved with love. In the great majority of situations in the Sangha we do not need to draw on the precepts. Love, understanding, and compassion can undo the knots in most cases. The precepts are there to support us, to remind us of the beautiful and wholesome direction in which we would most like to go. Using the offense of a precept to help resolve a situation is only a last resort when dealing with difficulties in the Sangha. First we should try every other possible method, including listening deeply, nourishing the wholesome qualities in the one who is having a difficulty, sharing our own experience of transforming difficulties, and providing concrete suggestions for overcoming obstacles on the path of practice. When we do invoke the precepts, it is always done in the spirit of supporting, embracing, and deeply understanding our brother or sister in order to help him or her to transform. The precepts are never used to punish, to reprimand, or to hurt members of the Sangha.

The second aim of the precepts is to protect and train individual monks and nuns, so that they have happiness and freedom. If a precept does not have this function, there is no need for it. A precept that cannot protect the Sangha and does not help a monk or a nun to have freedom, peace, and joy is not a necessary precept.

We have to look at the content of a precept and see if it protects both the Sangha and the individual monks and nuns. If it doesn't have these two effects, why should we keep it? Looking deeply, we can see the clear interdependence of these two aims. Protecting the Sangha enables the continuation of the community where individual monks, nuns, and laypeople can find a place to practice and take refuge. Protecting the integrity, peace, joy, and freedom of the individual ensures the continuity and strength of the whole community.

The Buddha did not give us precepts so that we would be caught in their outer form. If we do not understand clearly how a precept can protect the Sangha or our practice as a monk or a nun, we should ask our elder brothers and sisters to help us to look more deeply. This is why every monk and nun in the temple has an elder brother or sister as a mentor until the time he or she becomes a Dharma Teacher. The younger monks and nuns rely on the experience and understanding of their elders who have practiced before them. In addition, they must use their own powers of mindfulness, concentration, and insight to understand the content and aim of the precepts. In this way, monks and nuns will not practice blindly. If we practice them with understanding and love, the precepts will truly bring us more peace, more joy, and more freedom.

Recitation Ceremony of the Bhikshu Precepts

OPENING THE CEREMONY

Namo Tassa Bhagavato Arahato Samma Sambuddhassa
Namo Tassa Bhagavato Arahato Samma Sambuddhassa
Namo Tassa Bhagavato Arahato Samma Sambuddhassa
[Bell]

The Vinaya is deep and lovely.
We now have a chance to see, study,
and practice it.
We vow to realize its true meaning. [Bell]

IN THE PRESENCE of the Buddhas, the precious Dharma, and the Mahasangha we bow our heads. Today we shall recite the Pratimoksha so that the true teachings can remain in the world for a long time. The precepts are like the ocean. One lifetime alone is not enough to study and practice them. The precepts are like precious treasures. We never grow tired in their pursuit.

It is because we want to protect our sacred inheritance of the true teachings that we have gathered today to hear the recitation of the precepts. We have gathered as a Sangha to recite the precepts because we do not want to transgress the Four Degradation Offenses, the Twenty-seven Sangha Restoration Offenses, the Thirty-two Release and Expression of Regret Offenses, the One Hundred and Ten Expression of Regret Offenses, the Seventy Fine Manners Offenses, and the Seven Ways of Putting an End to Disputes. The Buddhas Vipashyin, Shikhin, Vishvabhu, Krakucchanda, Kanakamuni, Kashyapa, and Shakyamuni have devised these precepts for us to practice.

Let us receive, study, protect, and enrich them with the greatest respect, so that the Pratimoksha becomes more and more appropriate to our time, always maintaining the lifeblood of the true teachings. Now I will recite the Pratimoksha for the whole Sangha to hear.

Someone who is lame is not able to walk very far. The same is true of someone who transgresses the precepts. He cannot progress on the spiritual path. If we wish to go forward on the path of transformation, healing, and awakening we should practice the precepts wholeheartedly. The one who has not observed the precepts will become anxious. He is like a carriage on a rough and uneven road that will easily lose its axle-pin and the axle will be broken.

Reciting the precepts is like looking into a clear mirror to see ourselves. If the image is beautiful, we are happy; if it is ugly, we worry. If our precepts' body is clear, we are happy. If it is damaged, we worry. Reciting the precepts is like joining battle. If we are courageous we will go forward, if we are afraid we will run away. When our precepts' body is clear, we are confident and at peace. When it is damaged, we are anxious. In a truly democratic society, the people hold the highest position. On the Earth, the ocean is vaster than all lakes and rivers. Among the Holy Ones, the Buddha has the highest awakening. Of all spiritual laws and regulations, the Vinaya is the highest. The Buddha has devised the Pratimoksha for us to recite once every two weeks. [Bell]

Sanghakarman Procedure

SANGHAKARMAN MASTER: Has the whole community of bhikshus assembled?

SANGHA CONVENER: The whole community of bhikshus has assembled.

SANGHAKARMAN MASTER: Is there harmony in the community?

SANGHA CONVENER: Yes, there is harmony.

SANGHAKARMAN MASTER: Have those who have not yet received the bhikshu ordination already left?

SANGHA CONVENER: Those who have not yet received the bhikshu ordination have already left.

SANGHAKARMAN MASTER: Is there anyone who is absent, has asked to be represented, and has sent word that he has kept the precepts?

SANGHA CONVENER: No, there is not.

[In the case that someone is absent, we should say: Bhikshu _____ because of health reasons is not able to be present at the recitation. He has asked Bhikshu _____ to represent him and sends word that he has kept the precepts.]

SANGHAKARMAN MASTER: Has a representative of the Bhikshuni Sangha been sent today to request teachings?

SANGHA CONVENER: [One can either reply: Yes, Bhikshuni _____ has been sent or No, no one has been sent.]

SANGHAKARMAN MASTER: Why has the community assembled today?

SANGHA CONVENER: The community has assembled today to realize the Sanghakarman Procedure of reciting the Pratimoksha.

SANGHAKARMAN MASTER: Noble Sangha of Bhikshus, please listen. Today, _____ in the year _____ has been declared to be the Precepts' Recitation day. The Sangha has gathered at the appointed time and is ready to recite the precepts in a spirit of harmony. Thus the recitation is in accordance with the Vinaya. Is the announcement of the Sanghakarman Procedure realized?

THE SANGHA: Realized.

[Bell]

Introduction to the Recitation of the Bhikshu Precepts

Venerable Bhikshus, I am about to recite the Bhikshu Pratimoksha. Please listen attentively and examine yourself with care. If you know that you have broken any one of the precepts, you should admit your offense. If you have not broken a precept you should remain silent. If you are silent it means that your precepts' body is clear. If anyone asks you at a later time, you should reply as you have replied today. During this recitation if you have broken a precept and, having been asked three times, you do not say so, you commit the offense of deliberately telling a lie. According to the teaching of the Buddha, deliberately lying is an obstacle to the realization of the path of liberation. If you are aware that you have broken a precept and you wish your precepts' body to be clear again, you need to admit your offense, express regret, and begin anew, and after having done so you will be at peace.

Venerable Bhikshus, I have finished reading the introduction to the Pratimoksha.

Now I am asking you: In our community of bhikshus, is everyone's precepts' body clear?

[The question is asked three times.]

The Venerable Bhikshus have remained silent. Therefore we know that in the Sangha everyone's precepts' body is clear. Let us be aware of this, recognize it, and give it our approval. [Bell]

RECITATION

Degradation Offenses (Parajika)

Venerable Bhikshus, these are the four major precepts, called Degradation Offenses (Parajika), to be recited once every two weeks.

THE FIRST PRECEPT:

A bhikshu who has sexual intercourse with another person, whether female or male, and whether that person has given consent or not, breaks the first of the Four Degradation Offenses, is no longer worthy to remain a bhikshu, and cannot participate in the activities of the Bhikshu Sangha.

THE SECOND PRECEPT:

A bhikshu who steals or violates the property of another, whether that property is privately or publicly owned, and if the value of the property is significant enough that he could be taken to court, breaks the second of the Four Degradation Offenses, is no longer worthy to remain a bhikshu, and cannot participate in the activities of the Bhikshu Sangha.

THE THIRD PRECEPT:

A bhikshu who takes the life of another person by deed, word, or intention, breaks the third of the Four Degradation Offenses, is no longer worthy to remain a bhikshu, and cannot participate in the activities of the Bhikshu Sangha.

THE FOURTH PRECEPT:

A bhikshu who claims that he has attained realizations on the spiritual path, which he has not in fact realized, breaks the fourth of the Four Degradation Offenses, is no longer worthy to remain a bhikshu, and cannot participate in the activities of the Bhikshu Sangha.

Venerable Bhikshus, I have finished reciting the Four Degradation Offenses. When a bhikshu transgresses any one of these four precepts he has failed in his career as a bhikshu and can no longer remain in the Bhikshu Sangha.

Now I am asking you: as far as these Four Degradation Offenses are concerned, is your precepts' body clear?

[The question is asked three times.]

The Venerable Bhikshus have remained silent. Therefore we know that in the Sangha everyone's precepts' body is clear. Let us be aware of this, recognize it, and give it our approval. [Bell]

Sangha Restoration Offenses (Sanghavashesha)

Venerable Bhikshus, these are the Twenty-seven Sangha Restoration Offenses (Sanghavashesha) to be recited once every two weeks.

1. A bhikshu who, when motivated by sexual desire, touches the body of a woman or a man, commits a Sangha Restoration Offense.

2. A bhikshu who, when motivated by sexual desire, uses words which have the effect of arousing a sexual feeling in the woman or man to whom he is talking, commits a Sangha Restoration Offense.

3. A bhikshu who, when motivated by sexual desire, tells a woman or a man that it would be a good thing for her or him to have sexual relations with him, commits a Sangha Restoration Offense.

4. A bhikshu who verbally or in writing makes a proposal to a nun or a monk to leave the monastic life along with him, commits a Sangha Restoration Offense.

5. A bhikshu who acts as a matchmaker or as a go-between, or makes the arrangements for a wedding between two people, commits a Sangha Restoration Offense.

6. A bhikshu who, out of anger or jealousy, falsely accuses another bhikshu of a Degradation Offense, with the intention of destroying that bhikshu's reputation, commits a Sangha Restoration Offense.

7. A bhikshu who, out of anger or jealousy, takes a small mistake of another bhikshu and magnifies it so that it seems to be a Degrada-

tion Offense, with the intention of destroying that bhikshu's reputation, commits a Sangha Restoration Offense.

8. A bhikshu who uses political power to oppress or threaten other members of the monks' Sangha, commits a Sangha Restoration Offense.

9. A bhikshu who becomes a member of a political party or a political organization, whether secretly or openly, commits a Sangha Restoration Offense.

10. A bhikshu who acts as a spy, taking information from the Sangha and giving it to a political party or a political organization, commits a Sangha Restoration Offense.

11. A bhikshu who receives payment from the government, a political party, or a political organization, commits a Sangha Restoration Offense.

12. A bhikshu who does not teach the Dharma to the other monks, does not allow them to visit other places to study the sutras and to have access to clear and effective methods of practice and, as a result, the monks' study and practice remains incorrect and ineffective, commits a Sangha Restoration Offense.

13. A bhikshu who has only briefly read or heard about a method of practice belonging to another school of Buddhism or another tradition and has not had a chance to study or put this method into practice, yet publicly speaks or writes an article opposing it, commits a Sangha Restoration Offense.

14. A bhikshu who says that he does not owe any gratitude to parents, teachers, friends, or benefactors, commits a Sangha Restoration Offense.

15. A bhikshu who cuts himself off from the Sangha to set up a hermitage or temple of his own, without the permission of the Sangha, commits a Sangha Restoration Offense.

16. A bhikshu who builds a hermitage or temple for himself without asking the Sangha about where or in what style he should build it, builds it larger than is necessary, and in such a way that it causes inconvenience to others or obstructs a road or path that people use, commits a Sangha Restoration Offense.

17. A bhikshu who, when building a hermitage or temple, becomes involved in a land dispute which leads to a lawsuit, commits a Sangha Restoration Offense.

18. A bhikshu who turns the practice of chanting the sutra into a way of earning money by quoting a price which should be paid to him for performing a ceremony or a funeral service, commits a Sangha Restoration Offense.

19. A bhikshu who uses money reserved for the material necessities of the Sangha for construction, while the monks in the temple do not have enough food, drink, or medicine, commits a Sangha Restoration Offense.

20. A bhikshu who lives in a careless and disorderly manner causing the laypeople's faith in the Three Jewels to diminish, after having been

Parallax Press publishes books on engaged Buddhism and the practice of mindfulness by Thich Nhat Hanh and other authors. As a division of the Unified Buddhist Church, we are committed to making these teachings accessible to everyone and preserving them for future generations. We believe that, in doing so, we help alleviate suffering and create a more peaceful world.

For our catalog, please send in this card or visit www.parallax.org.

Please print

Name _____

Address _____

City _____ State _____ Zip _____

Country _____

PARALLAX PRESS

PO Box 7355

Berkeley CA 94707

warned three times without listening deeply and changing his way, commits a Sangha Restoration Offense.

21. A bhikshu who spends all his time and energy in work, organization, and management with the result that he forgets that the aim of a monk is to practice to liberate himself and other beings from suffering, after having been warned three times without listening deeply and changing his way, commits a Sangha Restoration Offense.

22. A bhikshu who causes disharmony within the Sangha by his way of speaking and acting, after having been warned three times without listening deeply and changing his way, commits a Sangha Restoration Offense.

23. A bhikshu who contributes to forming conflicting groups within the Sangha, so that the energy of the practice and harmony of the Sangha goes down, thereby creating the danger of a split in the Sangha, after having been warned three times without listening deeply and changing his way, commits a Sangha Restoration Offense.

24. A bhikshu who contributes to forming a splinter group within the Sangha, thereby creating the danger of a split in the Sangha, after having been warned three times without listening deeply and changing his way, commits a Sangha Restoration Offense.

25. A bhikshu who, out of discontentment, using the support and power of the government, causes disharmony in the Sangha, and without the permission of the Sangha, cuts himself off from the Sangha and persuades other members of the Sangha to follow him

to set up a new community, after having been warned three times without listening deeply and changing his way, commits a Sangha Restoration Offense.

26. A bhikshu who refuses to listen to the advice and instruction of other bhikshus regarding his understanding and practice of the Sutra, the Vinaya, and the Shastra, saying that he does not want to be disturbed but to be left in peace, after having been warned three times without listening deeply and changing his way, commits a Sangha Restoration Offense.

27. A bhikshu who gives teachings or leads people in practices which are not in accord with the teachings of transformation, healing, and liberation presented in Buddhism, after having been warned three times without listening deeply and changing his way, commits a Sangha Restoration Offense.

Venerable Bhikshus, I have finished reciting the Twenty-seven Sangha Restoration Offenses. The first nineteen precepts are broken as soon as they are committed. The last eight precepts are broken when the bhikshu has been warned three times to no effect. A bhikshu who breaks one of these twenty-seven precepts and intentionally hides his offense, shall be subject to Dwelling Apart from the Sangha (Manatva) for as long as the time during which he hid the offense. After that he will practice six days of Beginning Anew before the Ceremony of Purifying the Offense.

Now I am asking you: as far as these Twenty-seven Sangha Restoration Offenses are concerned, is your precepts' body clear?

[The question is asked three times.]

The Venerable Bhikshus have remained silent. Therefore we know that in the Sangha everyone's precepts' body is clear. Let us be aware of this, recognize it, and give it our approval. [Bell]

Release and Expression of Regret Offenses (Naihsargika-Payantika)

Venerable Bhikshus, these are the Thirty-two Release and Expression of Regret Offenses (Naihsargika-Payantika), to be recited once every two weeks.

1. A bhikshu who keeps in his possession or uses tobacco or any kind of illegal drug which is considered to be a mind-altering substance, commits an offense which involves Release and Expression of Regret.

2. A bhikshu who keeps and trades in worldly novels, horror stories, or horoscope and fortune-telling materials, commits an offense which involves Release and Expression of Regret.

3. A bhikshu who keeps for himself or for others toxic cultural items such as worldly films, videotapes, music, and electronic games, commits an offense which involves Release and Expression of Regret.

4. A bhikshu who keeps a television, video player, karaoke player, electronic games' machine, or any other kind of equipment used for showing worldly films, listening to worldly music, or playing electronic games, commits an offense which involves Release and Expression of Regret.

5. A bhikshu who has a private e-mail account, except with the permission of the Sangha, commits an offense which involves Release and Expression of Regret.

6. A bhikshu who owns his own car or uses expensive, luxurious, or flashy and brightly colored cars or telephones, commits an offense which involves Release and Expression of Regret.

7. A bhikshu who thinks that money and possessions can guarantee his security and seeks ways to accumulate these things in such a way that they become an obstacle to his path of practice, commits an offense which involves Release and Expression of Regret.

8. A bhikshu who opens or keeps a bank account for his own use, except when he has the permission of his Sangha to study Buddhism abroad, commits an offense which involves Release and Expression of Regret.

9. A bhikshu who makes himself the sole manager of the properties of the monastery or a charitable organization, without being designated by the Sangha to do so, commits an offense which involves Release and Expression of Regret.

10. A bhikshu who uses the monastery budget or the budget of a charitable organization to give support to his relatives or friends without the consent of other members of the Sangha or the charitable organization, commits an offense which involves Release and Expression of Regret.

11. A bhikshu who lends money with interest, invests money, buys and sells stocks or shares, invests in land or real estate, or plays the lottery, commits an offense which involves Release and Expression of Regret.

12. A bhikshu who uses a rosary made of expensive or brightly colored gems or wears objects of gold, silver, or precious stones, even though they are a keepsake of a close relation, or has a dental implant or crown made of gold or silver for cosmetic purposes or to display his wealth, commits an offense which involves Release and Expression of Regret.

13. A bhikshu who buys and stores expensive antiques and cherishes them as precious belongings commits an offense which involves Release and Expression of Regret.

14. A bhikshu who keeps in his possession too many books, even if those books are sutras or connected to Buddhist studies, who is afraid to lend them to others and who refuses to entrust them to the Sangha library for communal use, commits an offense which involves Release and Expression of Regret.

15. A bhikshu who stores a large amount of cloth and does not hand it over to the community or share it with someone who needs it, commits an offense which involves Release and Expression of Regret.

16. A bhikshu who has more than three formal robes (the antaravasa, the uttarasangha, and the sanghati), more than three long robes (the ao trang and ao nhat binh), and more than three suits (vat ho) worn under the long robe (not counting work clothes, warm underwear, or coats for those living in cold places), and who refuses to hand the excess over to the Sangha for keeping for newly ordained members, commits an offense which involves Release and Expression of Regret.

17. A bhikshu who wears monastic robes made of translucent, shiny, silky, or colorful material or any kind of material which is sewn with golden thread or glittering beads, commits an offense which involves Release and Expression of Regret.

18. A bhikshu who makes monastic robes according to a fashionable design or in imitation of clothes worn by wealthy and powerful people rather than robes that reflect the spirit of monastic simplicity, commits an offense which involves Release and Expression of Regret.

19. A bhikshu who buys luxurious personal items, commits an offense which involves Release and Expression of Regret.

20. A bhikshu who keeps and wears expensive or fashionable slippers or shoes, commits an offense which involves Release and Expression of Regret.

21. A bhikshu who stores a significant amount of shampoo, laundry soap, toothpaste, towels, toothbrushes, or other toiletries and refuses to share them with the Sangha, commits an offense which involves Release and Expression of Regret.

22. A bhikshu who is admitted to a hospital for treatment and stays in an expensive, private room with unnecessary luxuries, commits an offense which involves Release and Expression of Regret.

23. A bhikshu who lies on a luxurious bed, commits an offense which involves Release and Expression of Regret.

24. A bhikshu who decorates his room in a luxurious way with many comforts like that of people in the world, commits an offense which involves Release and Expression of Regret.

25. A bhikshu who stores a significant amount of food or drink in his personal storage space and does not bring it out to share with the Sangha, commits an offense which involves Release and Expression of Regret.

26. A bhikshu who goes to laypeople, whether those people are related to him or not, and collects material objects and funds for his personal use, commits an offense which involves Release and Expression of Regret.

27. A bhikshu who uses an offering from a layperson not in accordance with the layperson's wishes and without informing the layperson, so that the layperson suffers or is unhappy and upset, commits an offense which involves Release and Expression of Regret.

28. A bhikshu who is only interested in growing crops or manufacturing things to sell, even if it is to create income for the monastery, and therefore neglects the Sangha practice schedule, commits an offense which involves Release and Expression of Regret.

29. A bhikshu who raises animals or fowl for entertainment or with the intention to sell them and make money, commits an offense which involves Release and Expression of Regret.

30. A bhikshu who keeps items which belong to the whole Sangha for his personal use or gives them to someone else without the per-

mission of the Sangha, commits an offense which involves Release and Expression of Regret.

31. A bhikshu who uses what belongs to the Sangha in a way that is contrary to the Sangha's wishes, causing discontent or disharmony in the Sangha, commits an offense which involves Release and Expression of Regret.

32. A bhikshu who uses Sangha resources in a wasteful manner, including money, water, electricity, telephone, car, and so on, commits an offense which involves Release and Expression of Regret.

Venerable Bhikshus, I have finished reciting the Thirty-two Release and Expression of Regret Offenses. A bhikshu who transgresses any one of these thirty-two precepts has to come before the Sangha or before three or two other bhikshus who represent the Sangha in order to release and hand back to the Sangha the money or materials which he has been keeping, and then express his regret and begin anew.

Now I am asking you: as far as these Thirty-two Release and Expression of Regret Offenses are concerned, is your precepts' body clear?

[The question is asked three times.]

The Venerable Bhikshus have remained silent. Therefore we know that in the Sangha everyone's precepts' body is clear. Let us be aware of this, recognize it, and give it our approval. [Bell]

Expression of Regret Offenses (Payantika)

Venerable Bhikshus, these are the One Hundred and Ten Expression of Regret Offenses (Payantika), to be recited once every two weeks.

1. A bhikshu who masturbates, except in a dream, commits an Expression of Regret Offense.

2. A bhikshu who makes an appointment to go outside the monastery alone with a laywoman or a nun, commits an Expression of Regret Offense.

3. A bhikshu who sits alone in a hidden or solitary place with a laywoman or a nun, commits an Expression of Regret Offense.

4. A bhikshu who sits alone in a car or on a boat with a laywoman or a nun except in the case of an emergency or with the permission of the Sangha, commits an Expression of Regret Offense.

5. A bhikshu who writes a letter or gives a gift to a laywoman or a nun in order to show his feeling of affection for her or to win her heart, commits an Expression of Regret Offense.

6. A bhikshu who is sick, and refuses to ask for help from his fellow monks or laymen but instead allows one or more nuns or laywomen to look after him and bring him food, commits an Expression of Regret Offense.

7. A bhikshu who makes a telephone call to someone of the opposite sex at night, except in an emergency when he has let his fellow prac-

titioners know that he is making this call, commits an Expression of Regret Offense.

8. A bhikshu who after having been reminded by four or more bhikshus that he is emotionally attached to another person, whether female or male, and who refuses to listen, denies it, tries to negate what they say, or expresses anger, commits an Expression of Regret Offense.

9. A bhikshu who intentionally watches animals copulating, commits an Expression of Regret Offense.

10. A bhikshu who tells stories about sexual relations which he has seen on films, read in books, or heard others tell, commits an Expression of Regret Offense.

11. A bhikshu who knows that a man has an incurable disease, is trying to avoid paying debts, has broken a criminal law, or does not have the agreement of his wife or children to ordain, and still allows that person to receive the Novice Precepts, commits an Expression of Regret Offense.

12. A bhikshu who knows that a novice monk is not yet twenty years old or has not been accepted by the Sangha as an ordinee and still allows him to receive the Bhikshu Precepts, commits an Expression of Regret Offense.

13. A bhikshu who has not changed his roommate after eight months, except with the permission of the Sangha, commits an Expression of Regret Offense.

14. A bhikshu who hits another person in anger or out of resentment commits an Expression of Regret Offense.

15. A bhikshu who swears himself to one of the three unwholesome destinies during an argument, such as by saying "If I am lying, I will go to hell," commits an Expression of Regret Offense.

16. A bhikshu who forces someone to swear an oath commits an Expression of Regret Offense.

17. A bhikshu who says what is not true, adds or omits important details, speaks vulgar words to insult others, or speaks words that cause hatred and division, commits an Expression of Regret Offense.

18. A bhikshu who argues angrily in a loud voice and is gently encouraged by another bhikshu that he should say no more but return to his breathing or go outside to practice walking meditation in order to guard his mind, and who does not listen and continues to argue in a loud voice, commits an Expression of Regret Offense.

19. A bhikshu who is offered guidance by a fellow practitioner concerning his shortcomings in the practice, and not only does not receive the guidance with gratitude and respect by joining his palms, but tries to find ways to defend himself, to avoid the subject, or to excuse himself by bringing up the shortcomings of others, commits an Expression of Regret Offense.

20. A bhikshu who repeatedly speaks in a way that indirectly refers to the wrongdoing done in the past by another bhikshu, commits an Expression of Regret Offense.

21. A bhikshu who brings up another bhikshu's past offense, although the bhikshu has already been cleared of that offense with a Sanghakarman Procedure, commits an Expression of Regret Offense.

22. A bhikshu who interrogates or reprimands other monks in the Sangha in the presence of laypeople or during a meal, putting them in a difficult situation, commits an Expression of Regret Offense.

23. A bhikshu who threatens or frightens another bhikshu in such a way that the other becomes fearful and loses his motivation, commits an Expression of Regret Offense.

24. A bhikshu who is requested to come and resolve a conflict with someone and continuously finds ways to avoid being present to make the reconciliation, commits an Expression of Regret Offense.

25. A bhikshu who refuses to accept someone else's apology, commits an Expression of Regret Offense.

26. A bhikshu who allows his anger to continue up to seven days and still has no intention to practice reconciliation and Beginning Anew, commits an Expression of Regret Offense.

27. A bhikshu who, out of hatred or discrimination, repeatedly and aggressively disputes in words or writing with other ideologies or religious faiths instead of devoting himself to his studies and practice, commits an Expression of Regret Offense.

28. A bhikshu who, because of resentment with his fellow practitioners, does not seek help from the Sangha to find ways of reconciliation and instead leaves the community to go somewhere else or goes to

stay with his family for a while and then comes back again, commits an Expression of Regret Offense.

29. A bhikshu who does not practice to restore communication with his fellow practitioners but only complains to laypeople about difficulties and conflicts in the Sangha, commits an Expression of Regret Offense.

30. A bhikshu who does not use loving speech and deep listening to resolve the difficulties and disputes that have arisen between him and another monk, but instead only goes to complain to and seek an ally in one person after another, commits an Expression of Regret Offense.

31. A bhikshu who, upon hearing another monk complain about his difficulties with a third monk, makes no effort to bring about reconciliation between them, and instead allies himself with the monk who has complained to him in order to oppose the third monk, commits an Expression of Regret Offense.

32. A bhikshu who goes to another monastery and talks about the shortcomings and weaknesses of his former monastery in a complaining and reproachful way, commits an Expression of Regret Offense.

33. A bhikshu who claims to be up to date with the modern way of life and looks down disrespectfully at his teacher for being outdated and out of touch, commits an Expression of Regret Offense.

34. A bhikshu who knows that the Sangha is about to meet to perform Sanghakarman Procedures, and who finds ways not to be present or

pretends to be unwell and does not ask to be represented, commits an Expression of Regret Offense.

35. A bhikshu who has already performed a Sanghakarman Procedure with the Sangha but is still annoyed and displeased about the meeting and tells someone else that he is against the Sanghakarman Procedure that has been realized, commits an Expression of Regret Offense.

36. A bhikshu who has formally asked someone to represent him at a Sangha meeting and afterwards, feeling regret, looks for ways to deny the resolution that has been realized by Sanghakarman Procedure, commits an Expression of Regret Offense.

37. A bhikshu who does not put into effect, or encourages someone else to not put into effect a resolution that has been taken by the Sangha under the Sanghakarman Procedure, commits an Expression of Regret Offense.

38. A bhikshu who knows that another bhikshu or bhikshuni has committed a Degradation Offense and, in order to bring disrepute on this person, tells someone else about it who is not a bhikshu or bhikshuni before the Sangha has performed the Sanghakarman Procedure to affirm the offense, commits an Expression of Regret Offense.

39. A bhikshu who talks about the faults of another monk when that monk is not present, except in the case of the practice of Shining Light, commits an Expression of Regret Offense.

40. A bhikshu who sees that a fellow monk is sick and does not ask about his condition and look after him or find someone else to look after him, commits an Expression of Regret Offense.

41. A bhikshu who has been assigned by the Sangha to distribute items among Sangha members, but out of favoritism gives more to some monks and less to others, or refuses to give anything to a monk with whom he does not get along well, commits an Expression of Regret Offense.

42. A bhikshu who closes his eyes before suffering within himself and in the world and only takes comfort in laypeople's offerings, forgetting that the aim of the practice is to find ways to transform suffering into peace and joy, after having been warned by three other bhikshus without listening deeply and changing his way, commits an Expression of Regret Offense.

43. A bhikshu who sees that his fellow practitioner is about to commit an offense and says nothing to dissuade him against it or to let other bhikshus know so they can dissuade him against it, commits an Expression of Regret Offense.

44. A bhikshu who is narrow-minded, attached to his views, and maintains that the knowledge he presently possesses is absolute and unchanging, refusing to be open to receive the viewpoints and insights of others, after having been warned by three other bhikshus and still refusing to alter his attitude, commits an Expression of Regret Offense.

45. A bhikshu who uses authority, bribery, threat, propaganda, or indoctrination to force others, including children, to adopt his view, who does not respect the right of others to be different or their freedom to choose what to believe and how to decide, after having been warned by three other bhikshus and still refusing to alter his attitude, commits an Expression of Regret Offense.

46. A bhikshu who has relatives who are monks or nuns and uses his authority to protect them when they act wrongly or seeks ways to give them priority or privilege commits an Expression of Regret Offense.

47. A bhikshu who relies on his sphere of influence due to the office he holds in the Sangha in order to overpower another bhikshu who is his senior in years of ordination commits an Expression of Regret Offense.

48. A bhikshu who uses his authority to force another bhikshu to take his side in opposing a proposal which is about to be realized by a Sanghakarman Procedure commits an Expression of Regret Offense.

49. A bhikshu who is attached to his title or position of seniority in the Sangha, and becomes angry or annoyed when someone does not address him according to his position or tells that person that they should correct their way of addressing him, commits an Expression of Regret Offense.

50. A bhikshu who only gives special treatment to his own disciples and fails to care for other students who come to ask him for mentorship, commits an Expression of Regret Offense.

51. A bhikshu who encourages another monk to take his side so that he can have more power to overtake fellow practitioners, commits an Expression of Regret Offense.

52. A bhikshu who encourages another monk to leave his teacher and root temple in order to set up his own hermitage or go to another monastery, commits an Expression of Regret Offense.

53. A bhikshu who speaks in a sweet and exaggerating way to win someone's heart or complains and cries to arouse others' sympathy for himself, commits an Expression of Regret Offense.

54. A bhikshu who spreads news that he does not know to be certain or criticizes and condemns things of which he is not sure, in order to gain money, material benefits, or admiration for himself, commits an Expression of Regret Offense.

55. A bhikshu who, after having received donations from a layperson, defends that layperson and oppresses other monks or nuns, commits an Expression of Regret Offense.

56. A bhikshu who accepts disciples not with the purpose to teach and nurture them on the path of practice but only to serve his own reputation or his personal work, commits an Expression of Regret Offense.

57. A bhikshu who forces the monks to work hard growing crops, manufacturing things to sell, or performing spiritual services for money in order to increase the income of the monastery and thus does not allow them enough time for their studies and practice, commits an Expression of Regret Offense.

58. A bhikshu who pretends that he has a serious illness in order to be cared for by donors or to receive donations commits an Expression of Regret Offense.

59. A bhikshu who takes advantage of charitable organizations associated with the temple in order to gather additional possessions for himself or his monastery, commits an Expression of Regret Offense.

60. A bhikshu who criticizes and looks down on an offering made by a donor to the Sangha, commits an Expression of Regret Offense.

61. A bhikshu who accepts offerings from laypeople but does not truly practice to transform himself and says that it is the duty of laypeople to bring him offerings, commits an Expression of Regret Offense.

62. A bhikshu who goes to a nunnery to complain about his lack of material resources in order to receive an offering, commits an Expression of Regret Offense.

63. A bhikshu who only meets with people who are rich or intellectual, and out of discrimination does not show concern for those who are poor or uneducated, commits an Expression of Regret Offense.

64. A bhikshu who steals money or belongings of another person, tells someone else to steal them, or sees someone stealing them without finding ways to prevent it, commits an Expression of Regret Offense.

65. A bhikshu who breaks the promise he has made to a layperson and thus makes the person angry and critical of the monastic Sangha, commits an Expression of Regret Offense.

66. A bhikshu who avoids heavy work and looks for light work, except in the case of illness or if he is weak and has poor health, commits an Expression of Regret Offense.

67. A bhikshu who assesses the value of someone by the work he does, forgetting that the quality of a monk's practice is more important than the amount of work he accomplishes, commits an Expression of Regret Offense.

68. A bhikshu who is not aware that the responsibility of a monastic is to offer concrete practices which help people transform their suffering, but instead focuses all his energy on charitable works, forcing the Sangha to work so hard that they neglect their program of spiritual studies and practice, commits an Expression of Regret Offense.

69. A bhikshu who accepts hired work to earn some money for himself, not recognizing that his monastery already has the resources to support his material needs and spiritual studies and practice, commits an Expression of Regret Offense.

70. A bhikshu who tells people's fortunes (by reading palms, astrology, or other means) or burns paper money for the deceased in order to earn some money, commits an Expression of Regret Offense.

71. A bhikshu who eats a non-vegetarian meal, even though he excuses himself by saying that he lacks nutrition, commits an Expression of Regret Offense.

72. A bhikshu who neglects the practice activities of the Sangha in order to produce luxurious and fancy dishes using expensive ingredients, without considering that so many people in the world are suffering

from hunger and forgetting that he has committed himself to live the simple life of a monk, commits an Expression of Regret Offense.

73. A bhikshu who eats apart from the Sangha and eats in his room, except when he is sick or is unable to eat with the Sangha due to Sangha service, commits an Expression of Regret Offense.

74. A bhikshu who drinks beer, wine, or liquor of any kind, or takes any other substance that causes inebriation, except for medicinal use with the permission of the Bhikshu Sangha, commits an Expression of Regret Offense.

75. A bhikshu who enters a bar or a dimly lit coffee shop to have a drink or to sit and watch people come and go, commits an Expression of Regret Offense.

76. A bhikshu who goes to a layperson's house or a restaurant to attend a birthday party, an engagement reception, or a wedding reception, commits an Expression of Regret Offense.

77. A bhikshu who celebrates his birthday in a layperson's house or a restaurant, commits an Expression of Regret Offense.

78. A bhikshu who goes as a spectator to sports games, cinema, or worldly concerts commits an Expression of Regret Offense.

79. A bhikshu who rents and watches videos, or reads books and magazines which have a toxic effect, watering the seeds of sexual desire, fear, violence, sentimental weakness, and depression, commits an Expression of Regret Offense.

80. A bhikshu who watches television programs which have a toxic effect, watering the seeds of sexual desire, fear, violence, sentimental weakness, and depression, commits an Expression of Regret Offense.

81. A bhikshu who goes on to the Internet alone without another monk next to him as a protection against getting lost in toxic Websites commits an Expression of Regret Offense.

82. A bhikshu who consumes images or sounds which excite sexual desire from the Internet or the telephone, commits an Expression of Regret Offense.

83. A bhikshu who listens to or performs songs or music that is sad, sentimental, romantic, or exciting (such as rock music), commits an Expression of Regret Offense.

84. A bhikshu who plays electronic games, including those on a mobile phone or a computer, commits an Expression of Regret Offense.

85. A bhikshu who gambles or bets on horse races, car races, and other sports, commits an Expression of Regret Offense.

86. A bhikshu who drives in a careless and dangerous manner, speeding, swerving between cars, recklessly passing other cars, accelerating too quickly, or racing with another car, commits an Expression of Regret Offense.

87. A bhikshu who marches down the street clapping his hands, shouting, waving a flag, or throwing flowers to show support for a sports team, commits an Expression of Regret Offense.

88. A bhikshu who goes to watch military drills or preparations for battle, people fighting or arguing with each other, a martial art performance, or a magic show, commits an Expression of Regret Offense.

89. A bhikshu who goes to watch animals fighting or provokes animals to fight with each other, commits an Expression of Regret Offense.

90. A bhikshu who abuses animals or takes their bones, horns, or skin to create artwork or decorations, commits an Expression of Regret Offense.

91. A bhikshu who does not cultivate compassion and learn ways to protect the lives of animals, who kills an animal himself, gives consent for an animal to be killed, or does not prevent someone else from killing an animal, commits an Expression of Regret Offense.

92. A bhikshu who pollutes the environment, by burning and destroying forests or by using toxic chemicals, for example, commits an Expression of Regret Offense.

93. A bhikshu who intentionally allows his hair and beard to grow long, commits an Expression of Regret Offense.

94. A bhikshu who is not aware that the true beauty of a monk is found in his solidity and freedom, and instead spends too much time and care in dressing himself in order to create an outer show of attractiveness, commits an Expression of Regret Offense.

95. A bhikshu who when going into a town, village, or market wears lay clothing or a wig, commits an Expression of Regret Offense.

96. A bhikshu who separates himself from the Sangha and rents his own lodgings, commits an Expression of Regret Offense.

97. A bhikshu who sleeps overnight in a layperson's house, even for Sangha service, and at least one other male practitioner does not accompany him, except in special circumstances with the permission of the Sangha, commits an Expression of Regret Offense.

98. A bhikshu who stays longer than one week in a layperson's house, except with the permission of the Sangha, commits an Expression of Regret Offense.

99. A bhikshu who commits himself to a special relationship with a layperson by asking that person to be his father, mother, brother, sister, son, daughter, or grandchild, commits an Expression of Regret Offense.

100. A bhikshu who undertakes a course of study with the purpose of being awarded a bachelor's degree, master's degree, or doctorate in engineering, medicine, pharmacy, or other worldly subjects, except in the case that the course is in Buddhist studies, commits an Expression of Regret Offense.

101. A bhikshu who spends all his time studying worldly subjects, therefore neglecting to learn spiritual teachings and practice, commits an Expression of Regret Offense.

102. A bhikshu who immerses himself in and is carried away by his work and as a result fails to maintain good relationships between himself and other members of the Sangha, commits an Expression of Regret Offense.

103. A bhikshu who leaves his mentor before he has completed his fifth Rains' Retreat, or even after this time if his practice is still weak, commits an Expression of Regret Offense.

104. A bhikshu who does not complete the three-month Rains' Retreat once a year, commits an Expression of Regret Offense.

105. A bhikshu who goes outside the officially declared boundaries of the Rains' Retreat for an equal or greater number of days than he is within these boundaries, even if his reason for going outside is to teach, study, or do charitable work, commits an Expression of Regret Offense.

106. A bhikshu who transmits the Bhikshu Precepts without yet completing ten Rains' Retreats, commits an Expression of Regret Offense.

107. A bhikshu who has not mastered the Vinaya and who performs a Sanghakarman Procedure or makes the affirmation of an offense in a way which is not in accordance with the Vinaya, thus causing the Sangha to lose its peace, joy, and harmony, commits an Expression of Regret Offense.

108. A bhikshu who complains about the precepts and fine manners, saying that the articles presented are bothersome, too complicated, too detailed, not truly necessary, or that they take away one's freedom, commits an Expression of Regret Offense.

109. A bhikshu who does not recite the Pratimoksha with the Sangha at least once in three months, unless he has a long-lasting and serious illness, commits an Expression of Regret Offense.

110. A bhikshu who has not yet begun to study the Classical Pratimoksha in parallel with the Revised Pratimoksha after one year of receiving the full ordination, commits an Expression of Regret Offense.

Venerable Bhikshus, I have finished reciting the One Hundred and Ten Expression of Regret Offenses. A bhikshu who transgresses any one of these one hundred and ten precepts has to express his regret and begin anew before three or two bhikshus in order to make his precepts' body clear.

Now I am asking you, as far as these One Hundred and Ten Expression of Regret Offenses are concerned, is your precept's body clear?

[The question is asked three times.]

The Venerable Bhikshus have remained silent. Therefore we know that in the Sangha everyone's precepts' body is clear. Let us be aware of this, recognize it, and give it our approval. [Bell]

Fine Manners Offenses (Shaiksha)

Venerable Bhikshus, these are the Seventy Fine Manners Offenses (Shaiksha), to be recited once every two weeks.

1. A bhikshu should not talk, laugh, joke, whistle, sing, shout to someone far off, chew his food, use a toothpick, or talk on the telephone while walking.

2. A bhikshu, while walking, should not join his palms in greeting, snap his fingers, swing his arms, sway his body, move his arms and legs as if he were dancing, skip, turn his face up to the sky, or walk in haste.

3. A bhikshu, while walking, should not be putting on clothes or adjusting his robe.

4. A bhikshu, while walking, should not drag or stamp his feet, nor take very long strides.

5. A bhikshu should not speak in such a way to probe into someone's personal life to discover his faults. He should not speak with a sharp, sarcastic, or rough voice, nor should he interrupt someone who is speaking.

6. A bhikshu should practice to speak softly and slowly, not talking too fast and swallowing his words. He should not speak so loudly that his voice drowns the voices of others.

7. A bhikshu should not tell ghost or horror stories which water the seeds of fear in another person.

8. A bhikshu should not imitate someone else's way of speaking or manner in order to make fun of that person.

9. A bhikshu should not laugh too loudly, open his mouth too wide, nor yawn or pick his teeth without covering his mouth.

10. A bhikshu should not squat. He should sit solidly and at ease with his back upright, without shaking his legs or swinging or tapping his feet.

11. A bhikshu should not sit in a place where people are drinking alcohol, eating meat, gambling, using abusive language, disrespectfully teasing each other, or speaking badly about others.

12. A bhikshu should practice lying on his right side to go to sleep as this is the most peaceful and healthy position.

13. A bhikshu should not lie down in a place where people pass by, nor should he read or chant the sutras when lying down, except in special cases.

14. A bhikshu should not stand with his hands on his hips, nor should he hold his hands behind his back.

15. A bhikshu should not choose only the best tasting food for himself.

16. A bhikshu, while eating, should not talk and should not chew and swallow his food in a rush. He should chew each mouthful slowly about thirty times before swallowing.

17. A bhikshu should not chew and slurp loudly, lick the food from his bowl or plate with his tongue, nor should he open his mouth too wide when putting food into it.

18. A bhikshu should not put down his empty bowl when those who have been ordained longer than him are still eating in a formal meal. He should not stand up in the middle of the meal, nor stand up as soon as he has finished eating, before the sound of the bell.

19. A bhikshu should not leave leftover food when he is finished eating.

20. A bhikshu should eat lightly in the evening so that he feels light in body and avoids wasting time cooking.

21. A bhikshu should not buy luxurious and expensive food items, such as tea, sweets and so on, except in special cases.

22. A bhikshu should care for his alms bowl with respect and should not use more than one alms bowl.

23. A bhikshu should not make noise with his spoon or chopsticks against his alms bowl.

24. A bhikshu should always be neatly dressed wearing his long robe when he goes outside the monastery.

25. A bhikshu should dry his undergarments in the designated place.

26. A bhikshu should not dress untidily or wear dirty robes and should bathe regularly enough so that his body does not have odors.

27. A bhikshu should exercise regularly so that he remains strong and healthy and should learn the way to conserve the three energies (sexual, breath, and spirit.)

28. A bhikshu should clean his teeth after every meal and while cleaning his teeth should not walk back and forth, talk, laugh, or joke.

29. A bhikshu should not sleep on the same bed as a layman, except in special circumstances for which he has informed the other bhikshus.

30. A bhikshu should not sleep on the same bed with another monk. In the case in which there are not enough beds, it is possible to share a bed temporarily, but they should not use the same blanket. In the case in which there is no other option and they have to share a blanket, they should be fully clothed.

31. A bhikshu should not sleep without wearing a shirt and should not sleep wearing only shorts.

32. A bhikshu who has a nightmare should not allow himself to go back to sleep immediately, but should sit up and massage so that the blood circulates evenly, or practice walking meditation outside for ten minutes before going back to sleep. If he has a seminal emission while sleeping, he should rise early to take a shower and change his clothes so that he is on time for the early morning sitting and chanting.

33. A bhikshu should not join his palms to bow in a mechanical way, without mindfulness. When receiving an offering, he should bow, joining his palms like a lotus bud.

34. A bhikshu should practice looking deeply while touching the earth, not just prostrating mechanically, and while in this position his four limbs and forehead should touch the ground.

35. A bhikshu should not urinate or defecate near a stupa or shrine, in a place which is not shielded from view, in a vegetable plot, or in a flowing body of water.

36. A bhikshu should knock slowly three times before entering someone else's room.

37. A bhikshu should not leave his shoes or slippers untidily, but should leave them neatly in a straight line.

38. A bhikshu should neatly arrange and tidy everything when he is finished using it.

39. A bhikshu should not leave his clothes soaking for a long period of time without washing and drying them so that they do not disintegrate in a short time.

40. A bhikshu, before inviting the sound of any bell, should breathe in and out mindfully three times and recite the gatha for inviting the bell. When he hears the sound of the bell, he should stop all thinking, speech, and movement, and practice mindful breathing.

41. A bhikshu should respect the schedule of the Sangha by being present and arriving on time for all activities so that he may be a model for his fellow practitioners.

42. A bhikshu should not arrive in the Dharma Hall after the teacher has arrived and should not leave in the middle of the Dharma talk.

While listening to a recording of a Dharma talk he should sit upright, listening with all his attention and respect as he would in the Dharma Hall.

43. A bhikshu, when hearing the telephone ring, should give rise to mindfulness, returning to his breathing for at least three breaths before picking up the telephone. He should use the telephone only for necessary conversations, sitting in an upright posture, using loving speech, and without speaking too loudly, teasing, or joking.

44. A bhikshu, upon hearing the person on the other end of the line making unnecessary conversation, should find a way to politely excuse himself before hanging up the telephone.

45. A bhikshu should not use a portable telephone during sitting or walking meditation, sutra chanting, Sangha meetings, or study classes.

46. A bhikshu, while bathing, should not sing, recite the sutras, talk loudly, tease, or joke.

47. A bhikshu, while cooking or working, should practice mindfulness just as he does during sitting meditation or other Dharma practices and should move around in a calm manner, without rushing.

48. A bhikshu who is given a special task by the Sangha should not use it in such a way to give him authority or consider that his work is more important than others' work. He should be aware that all kinds of work done to serve the Sangha are equally important.

49. A bhikshu, when receiving a task from the Sangha, no matter how important it is, should always do it with ease and freedom, not tak-

ing advantage of it to unnecessarily excuse himself from activities of the Sangha.

50. A bhikshu should not take on more work beyond his capability or state of health. He should not be afraid of inconveniencing others and accept more work, which will then make him anxious, tired, and dispirited.

51. A bhikshu who is studying teachings of a profound, metaphysical, and mystical nature, should constantly ask himself how he may apply these teachings in his daily life to transform his suffering and realize liberation.

52. A bhikshu should not read books and sutras without applying the basic and essential practices of Buddhism in order to transform his afflictions and habit energies.

53. A bhikshu, in addition to reading books on Buddhism, should also read books on the history of civilizations of the world, general history and teachings of other religious faiths, applied psychology, and the most recent scientific discoveries. These areas of knowledge can help him to understand and share the teachings with people in a way that is appropriate to their situation.

54. A bhikshu should only ask to leave his Sangha and practice elsewhere when he sees that there are not enough conditions for his progress in his present situation. He should choose to go to a monastery where there is harmony and happiness in the Sangha.

55. A bhikshu, when he sees anger arising in himself, should not say or do anything, but practice mindful breathing, not continuing to lis-

ten and give attention to the person whom he thinks is the cause of his anger. If necessary he may go outside to practice walking meditation to look deeply, recognizing that the main cause of his anger is the seed of anger within himself.

56. A bhikshu should have another monk as a second body to look after and support, just as he himself is the second body of another monk who supports and looks after him.

57. A bhikshu should not go outside the monastery at night, except in an emergency. If he does have to go outside, he should let the Sangha know and another monk should accompany him.

58. A bhikshu should bring one formal robe with him if he has to be away from his monastery overnight.

59. A bhikshu, while driving, should not make unnecessary conversation, tease, joke, talk on the telephone, or read the map. He should not drive his vehicle alongside another vehicle to hold a conversation with the driver of the other vehicle nor honk the horn of his car in irritation at another vehicle. He should not drive faster than the official speed limit.

60. A bhikshu, while driving, should wear his seat belt, should have his driver's license and the official papers of the car he is driving with him. When getting into a car or onto a motorbike he should arrange his robes so that they do not hang outside the car or get stuck in the wheel of the motorbike.

61. A bhikshu who is driving on a long trip and begins to feel sleepy or tired, should ask someone else to drive. If there is no one to replace

him, he should stop the car and rest until he feels refreshed and awake, aware that the lives of the passengers in the car he is driving depend on his careful attention.

62. A bhikshu should not go into a shop or area where toxic books, magazines, and posters are displayed or sold.

63. A bhikshu should not tease and joke with a vendor.

64. A bhikshu who, going outside of the monastery, meets a high monk or nun of his own tradition should stop, join his palms, and exchange greetings with him or her. If he meets a monk or nun of a different tradition, he should do the same.

65. A bhikshu should not visit his family more frequently than the Sangha's guidelines allow. He may regularly write home to his family, sharing his happiness and spiritual practice so that his family's happiness and faith in the practice will increase. He should not tell his family about the difficulties he encounters in his life as a monk in such a way that they become concerned and anxious about him.

66. A bhikshu, when helping to resolve difficult situations in his family, should use his energy of mindfulness and share the practices of deep listening and loving speech.

67. A bhikshu, when visiting his family, should not keep asking for one thing after another, and when his family gives him something, he should share it with the Sangha.

68. A bhikshu, when receiving and talking with visiting laypeople in the monastery, should refrain from taking part in conversations about

worldly matters containing blame, criticism, or discrimination. Rather he should listen deeply to the lay practitioner's suffering, and using his own experience in the practice, should offer concrete practices which will help the lay practitioner transform himself as well as the situation in his family and society.

69. A bhikshu, when receiving and talking with visiting laypeople in the monastery, should not listen to tales about the shortcomings of other practice centers or monks or nuns from other temples.

70. A bhikshu should not try to find ways to be in close contact only with people who are powerful, wealthy, or famous.

Venerable Bhikshus, I have finished reciting the Seventy Fine Manners Offenses (Shaiksha). A bhikshu who transgresses any one of these seventy offenses should know that his practice is still weak. He should give rise to a feeling of remorse and promise to his mentor that he will practice more solidly.

Now I am asking you: as far as these Seventy Fine Manners Offenses are concerned, have you practiced with stability?

[The question is asked three times.]

The Venerable Bhikshus have remained silent. Therefore we know that in the Sangha the fine manners have been practiced with stability. Let us be aware of this, recognize it, and give it our approval. [Bell]

Seven Ways of Putting an End to Disputes

Venerable Bhikshus, these are the Seven Ways of Putting an End to Disputes (Sapta dhikarana-shamatha-dharma), to be recited once every two weeks.

1. If a meeting of the Sangha is needed with the presence of those who are involved in the dispute so that they can talk about the injustice and suffering they have experienced, and during this meeting the Sangha can practice deep and compassionate listening in order to relieve the suffering of both sides, then let the Sangha call such a meeting to resolve the dispute.

2. If a meeting is needed to encourage those involved in the dispute to recall and tell what they have seen, heard, and thought about the dispute in the spirit of deep listening and loving speech, then let such a meeting be called to resolve the dispute.

3. If a meeting is needed to affirm that a person involved in the dispute was going through a mental crisis or illness at the time of the dispute and did not know that he was causing difficulties and making others suffer, and now that the crisis is over he still cannot remember well what happened, then let such a meeting be called to resolve the dispute.

4. If a meeting is needed to give those who are involved in the dispute an opportunity to recognize and acknowledge their own unskillfulness and lack of mindfulness, wherein one person first expresses his unskillfulness, lack of mindfulness, and regrets using loving speech,

and then the other person(s) will be encouraged to do the same, helping to de-escalate the conflict, then let such a meeting be called to resolve the dispute.

5. If a meeting is needed to appoint a committee to investigate and study the causes and nature of the dispute, and after investigating this committee should present a report to the Sangha so that they can resolve the dispute, then let such a meeting be called to resolve the dispute.

6. If a meeting is needed to resolve the dispute by means of a majority vote, since the dispute has gone on so long unresolved, and after the decision by majority is made no one can bring the matter up again, then let such a meeting be called to resolve the dispute.

7. If a meeting in the presence of the most respected elders of the community is needed to resolve a dispute and in this meeting the elders will declare a general amnesty, encouraging everyone to use their compassion to put an end to resentment, like laying straw on the mud, then let such a meeting be called to resolve the dispute.

Venerable Bhikshus, I have finished reciting the Seven Ways of Putting an End to Disputes.

Now I am asking you: has everyone in the Sangha studied, practiced, and observed these Seven Ways of Putting an End to Disputes?

[The question is asked three times.]

The Venerable Bhikshus are silent. Therefore we know that in the Sangha everyone has studied, practiced and observed these Seven Ways of Putting an End to Disputes. Let us be aware of this, recognize it, and give it our approval. [Bell]

CONCLUSION

Venerable Bhikshus, I have finished reciting the 250 Bhikshu Precepts, including the Four Degradation Offenses, the Twenty-seven Sangha Restoration Offenses, the Thirty-two Release and Expression of Regret Offenses, the One Hundred and Ten Expression of Regret Offenses, the Seventy Fine Manners Offenses, and the Seven Ways of Putting an End to Disputes. I wish to thank the Venerable Bhikshus for helping me to recite the precepts serenely.

[In the unusual circumstance that we cannot recite all 250 of the Bhikshu Precepts, we can use the following conclusion:

Venerable Bhikshus, I have finished reciting the Bhikshu Precepts, including the Four Degradation Offenses and _____ [list the precepts which were recited today]. You should read and study for yourself the remaining precepts so that your practice of the precepts can deepen and grow more extensive day by day. I wish to thank the Venerable Bhikshus for helping me to recite the precepts serenely.]

Venerable Bhikshus, now I will recite the Four Objects of Refuge and the Four Ways of Meeting with Certain Situations, the essential practices that have been devised by the Buddha and transmitted to us from the Original Sangha of the Buddha. Please listen wholeheartedly and put them into practice.

Here are the Four Objects of Refuge:

1. A bhikshu takes refuge in his sanghati robe as a bird relies on its wings.

2. A bhikshu takes refuge in his begging bowl in order to practice humility, to have the opportunity to be in contact with laypeople and to help them realize awakening.

3. A bhikshu takes refuge in the foot of a tree, a hermitage, or a monastery as his dwelling place, and never leaves his Sangha.

4. A bhikshu takes refuge in plants, herbs, and simple, wholesome foods in order to cure disease.

Here are the Four Ways of Meeting with Certain Situations:

1. A bhikshu who is insulted by someone, shall not insult that person in return.

2. A bhikshu whom someone is angry with, shall not be angry with that person in return.

3. A bhikshu who is belittled by someone, shall not belittle that person in return.

4. A bhikshu who is beaten by someone, shall not beat that person in return. [Bell]

Inspiring Verses by the Seven Buddhas

Buddha Vipashyin has taught:
Inclusiveness is the first practice.
Nirvana is the final aim.
To make others suffer
is not the practice of a monastic.

Buddha Shikhin has taught:
Someone whose eyes are bright
avoids perilous paths.
The wise ones in the world
do not fall into realms of suffering.

Buddha Vishvabhu has taught:
Not denigrating or envious of others,
practicing and observing the precepts,
eating and drinking with moderation,
diligently dwelling in peace,
this is what the Buddha teaches.

Buddha Krakucchanda has taught:
Just as when the bee visits the flower,
it does not destroy its fragrance and beauty,
but only removes the sweet nectar,
a bhikshu when going out into the world
practices like that.
He does not get caught in worldly matters.

He looks straight ahead, walks mindfully.

Buddha Kanakamuni has taught:
Someone who masters his mind,
walking steadily on the holy path,
has nothing to worry about,
since he dwells in mindfulness.

Buddha Kashyapa has taught:
Someone who does not cause others to suffer,
who is diligent in doing goodness,
purifies his mind.
This is what the Buddha teaches.

Buddha Shakyamuni has taught:
By guarding our actions of body and speech,
we purify our minds.
If you are able to do this,
you realize your nature of no-birth and no-death. [Bell]

Sharing the Merit

Venerable Bhikshus, please join your palms so that we can offer up the merit of our recitation together.

To respect and put into practice
the wonderful Pratimoksha,
to leave behind the world of birth and death
and be able to realize nirvana,
is to realize the highest happiness.

For as long as the precepts endure,
the teachings of the Buddha endure.
To recite and protect the precepts
means that the Buddha is always present,
forever in the world. [Bell]

Reciting the Vinaya,
practicing the way of awareness,
gives rise to benefits without limit.
We vow to share the fruits with all beings.
We vow to offer tribute to parents, teachers, friends, and numerous
    beings
who give guidance and support along the path.
[Bell] [Bell] [Bell]

Recitation Ceremony of the Bhikshuni Precepts

OPENING THE CEREMONY

Namo Tassa Bhagavato Arahato Samma Sambuddhassa
Namo Tassa Bhagavato Arahato Samma Sambuddhassa
Namo Tassa Bhagavato Arahato Samma Sambuddhassa
[Bell]

The Vinaya is deep and lovely.
We now have a chance to see, study,
and practice it.
We vow to realize its true meaning. [Bell]

IN THE PRESENCE of the Buddhas, the precious Dharma, and the Mahasangha we bow our heads. Today we shall recite the Pratimoksha so that the true teachings can remain in the world for a long time. The precepts are like the ocean. One lifetime alone is not enough to study and practice them. The precepts are like precious treasures. We never grow tired in their pursuit.

It is because we want to protect our sacred inheritance of the true teachings that we have gathered today to hear the recitation of the precepts. We have gathered as a Sangha to recite the precepts because we do not want to transgress the Eight Degradation Offenses, the Thirty-six Sangha Restoration Offenses, the Forty Release and Expression of Regret Offenses, the One Hundred and Forty-two Expression of Regret Offenses, the One Hundred and Fifteen Fine Manners Offenses and the Seven Ways of Putting an End to Disputes. The Buddhas Vipashyin, Shikhin, Vishvabhu, Krakucchanda, Kanakamuni, Kashyapa, and Shakyamuni have devised these precepts for us to practice.

Let us receive, study, protect, and enrich them with the greatest respect, so that the Pratimoksha becomes more and more appropriate to our time, always maintaining the lifeblood of the true teachings. Now I will recite the Pratimoksha for the whole Sangha to hear.

Someone who is lame is not able to walk very far. The same is true of someone who transgresses the precepts. She cannot progress on the spiritual path. If we wish to go forward on the path of transformation, healing, and awakening we should practice the precepts wholeheartedly. The one who has not observed the precepts will become anxious. She is like a carriage on a rough and uneven road that will easily lose its axle-pin and the axle will be broken.

Reciting the precepts is like looking into a clear mirror to see ourselves. If the image is beautiful, we are happy; if it is ugly, we worry. If our precepts' body is clear, we are happy. If it is damaged, we worry. Reciting the precepts is like joining battle. If we are courageous we will go forward, if we are afraid we will run away. When our precepts' body is clear, we are confident and at peace. When it is damaged, we are anxious. In a truly democratic society, the people hold the highest position. On the Earth, the ocean is vaster than all lakes and rivers. Among the Holy Ones, the Buddha has the highest awakening. Of all spiritual laws and regulations, the Vinaya is the highest. The Buddha has devised the Pratimoksha for us to recite once every two weeks. [Bell]

Sanghakarman Procedure

SANGHAKARMAN MASTER: Has the whole community of bhikshunis assembled?

SANGHA CONVENER: The whole community of bhikshunis has assembled.

SANGHAKARMAN MASTER: Is there harmony in the community?

SANGHA CONVENER: Yes, there is harmony.

SANGHAKARMAN MASTER: Have those who have not yet received the bhikshuni ordination already left?

SANGHA CONVENER: Those who have not yet received the bhikshuni ordination have already left.

SANGHAKARMAN MASTER: Is there anyone who is absent, has asked to be represented, and has sent word that she has kept the precepts?

SANGHA CONVENER: No, there is not.

[In the case that someone is absent, we should say: Bhikshuni _____ because of health reasons is not able to be present at the recitation. She has asked Bhikshuni _____ to represent her and sends word that she has kept the precepts.]

SANGHAKARMAN MASTER: Why has the community assembled today?

SANGHA CONVENER: The community has assembled today to realize the Sanghakarman Procedure of reciting the Pratimoksha.

SANGHAKARMAN MASTER: Noble Sangha of Bhikshunis, please listen. Today, _____ in the year _____ has been declared to be the Precepts' Recitation day. The Sangha has gathered at the appointed time and is ready to recite the precepts in a spirit of harmony. Thus the recitation is in accordance with the Vinaya. Is the announcement of the Sanghakarman Procedure realized?

THE SANGHA: Realized.
[Bell]

Introduction to the Recitation of the Bhikshuni Precepts

Venerable Bhikshunis, I am about to recite the Bhikshuni Pratimoksha. Please listen attentively and examine yourself with care. If you know that you have broken any one of the precepts, you should admit your offense. If you have not broken a precept you should remain silent. If you are silent it means that your precepts' body is clear. If anyone asks you at a later time, you should reply as you have replied today. During this recitation if you have broken a precept and, having been asked three times, you do not say so, you commit the offense of deliberately telling a lie. According to the teaching of the Buddha, deliberately lying is an obstacle to the realization of the path of liberation. If you are aware that you have broken a precept and you wish your precepts' body to be clear again, you need to admit your offense, express regret, and begin anew, and after having done so you will be at peace.

Venerable Bhikshunis, I have finished reading the introduction to the Pratimoksha.

Now I am asking you: In our community of bhikshunis, is everyone's precepts' body clear?

[The question is asked three times.]

The Venerable Bhikshunis have remained silent. Therefore we know that in the Sangha everyone's precepts' body is clear. Let us be aware of this, recognize it, and give it our approval.   [Bell]

RECITATION

Degradation Offenses (Parajika)

Venerable Bhikshunis, these are the eight major precepts, called Degradation Offenses (Parajika), to be recited once every two weeks.

THE FIRST PRECEPT:

A bhikshuni who has sexual intercourse with another person, whether male or female, and whether that person has given consent or not, breaks the first of the Eight Degradation Offenses, is no longer worthy to remain a bhikshuni, and cannot participate in the activities of the Bhikshuni Sangha.

THE SECOND PRECEPT:

A bhikshuni who steals or violates the property of another, whether that property is privately or publicly owned, and if the value of the property is significant enough that she could be taken to court, breaks the second of the Eight Degradation Offenses, is no longer worthy to remain a bhikshuni, and cannot participate in the activities of the Bhikshuni Sangha.

THE THIRD PRECEPT:

A bhikshuni who takes the life of another person by deed, word, or intention, breaks the third of the Eight Degradation Offenses, is no longer worthy to remain a bhikshuni, and cannot participate in the activities of the Bhikshuni Sangha.

THE FOURTH PRECEPT:

A bhikshuni who claims that she has attained realizations on the spiritual path, which she has not in fact realized, breaks the fourth of the Eight Degradation Offenses, is no longer worthy to remain a bhikshuni, and cannot participate in the activities of the Bhikshuni Sangha.

THE FIFTH PRECEPT:

A bhikshuni who is motivated by sexual desire, knowing that the other person, whether male or female, is also motivated by sexual desire, and intentionally touches the body of that person, breaks the fifth of the Eight Degradation Offenses, is no longer worthy to remain a bhikshuni, and cannot participate in the activities of the Bhikshuni Sangha.

THE SIXTH PRECEPT:

A bhikshuni who is motivated by sexual desire, knowing that the other person, whether male or female, is also motivated by sexual desire, and allows that person to hold her hand, to take hold of her robe, to walk alongside her, to stand alongside her, to lean against her while they are speaking, and arranges to meet in a deserted place with the idea of indulging in sexual relations, breaks the sixth of the Eight Degradation Offenses, is no longer worthy to remain a bhikshuni, and cannot participate in the activities of the Bhikshuni Sangha.

THE SEVENTH PRECEPT:

A bhikshuni who is intent upon having sexual relations with someone, whether male or female, and through word or gesture arouses sexual desire in that person, breaks the seventh of the Eight Degradation Offenses, is no longer worthy to remain a bhikshuni, and cannot participate in the activities of the Bhikshuni Sangha.

THE EIGHTH PRECEPT:

A bhikshuni who is intent upon having sexual relations with someone, whether male or female, and says to that person that she is willing to offer him or her sexual relations, breaks the eighth of the Eight Degradation Offenses, is no longer worthy to remain a bhikshuni, and cannot participate in the activities of the Bhikshuni Sangha.

Venerable Bhikshunis, I have finished reciting the Eight Degradation Offenses. When a bhikshuni transgresses any one of these eight precepts she has failed in her career as a bhikshuni and can no longer remain in the Bhikshuni Sangha.

Now I am asking you: as far as these Eight Degradation Offenses are concerned, is your precepts' body clear?

[The question is asked three times.]

The Venerable Bhikshunis have remained silent. Therefore we know that in the Sangha everyone's precepts' body is clear. Let us be aware of this, recognize it, and give it our approval. [Bell]

Sangha Restoration Offenses (Sanghavashesha)

Venerable Bhikshunis, these are the Thirty-six Sangha Restoration Offenses (Sanghavashesha) to be recited once every two weeks.

1. A bhikshuni who has an emotional attachment to another person, whether male or female, and finds ways to damage the reputation of the other person because her feelings are not reciprocated by the other, commits a Sangha Restoration Offense.

2. A bhikshuni who has an emotional attachment to another person, whether male or female, and thus manifests jealousy or anger when she sees the other person interacting with someone else, causing disturbance in the Sangha, commits a Sangha Restoration Offense.

3. A bhikshuni who has an emotional attachment to another person, whether male or female, who uses her authority to prohibit the other person from having a close relationship with anyone else, and tells others that they are not to have a close relationship with the person to whom she is attached, commits a Sangha Restoration Offense.

4. A bhikshuni who has an emotional attachment to another person, whether male or female, knowing that the other person has an emotional attachment with a third person, who does everything she can to separate them, and drives the third person out of the community, commits a Sangha Restoration Offense.

5. A bhikshuni who verbally or in writing makes a proposal to another monk or nun to leave the monastic life along with her, commits a Sangha Restoration Offense.

6. A bhikshuni who acts as a matchmaker or as a go-between, or makes the arrangements for a wedding between two people, commits a Sangha Restoration Offense.

7. A bhikshuni who, out of special affection for another bhikshuni, uses her authority to protect that bhikshuni, allowing her to remain in the nunnery even though the Sangha has decided that she should leave, commits a Sangha Restoration Offense.

8. A bhikshuni who, out of anger or jealousy, falsely accuses another bhikshuni of a Degradation Offense, with the intention of destroying that bhikshuni's reputation, commits a Sangha Restoration Offense.

9. A bhikshuni who conceals a Degradation Offense on the part of another bhikshuni, and waits until the other bhikshuni is dead, has disrobed, or has joined another religious order before revealing it to the Bhikshuni Sangha, commits a Sangha Restoration Offense.

10. A bhikshuni who, out of anger or jealousy, takes a small mistake of another bhikshuni and magnifies it so that it seems to be a Degradation Offense, with the intention of destroying that bhikshuni's reputation, commits a Sangha Restoration Offense.

11. A bhikshuni who knows that another bhikshuni or bhikshu has committed a Degradation Offense and, in order to bring disrepute on this person, tells someone else who is not a bhikshuni or bhikshu

about it before the Sangha has performed the Sanghakarman Procedure to affirm the offense, commits a Sangha Restoration Offense.

12. A bhikshuni who, out of anger, heavily punishes or mistreats another nun in her Sangha, causing that person to fall ill and be unable to continue in her studies or practice, commits a Sangha Restoration Offense.

13. A bhikshuni who, out of a grudge or resentment, uses her authority to force another bhikshuni to admit an offense which has no basis in reality and makes that bhikshuni leave the nunnery, which makes her suffer so much that she becomes discouraged and disrobes, commits a Sangha Restoration Offense.

14. A bhikshuni who, relying on the authority she holds due to her position in the congregation or her seniority, acts in an ill-mannered way that insults other nuns so that they suffer to such an extent that they lose heart in their studies and practice, commits a Sangha Restoration Offense.

15. A bhikshuni who uses political power to oppress or threaten other members of the nuns' Sangha, commits a Sangha Restoration Offense.

16. A bhikshuni who becomes a member of a political party or a political organization, whether secretly or openly, commits a Sangha Restoration Offense.

17. A bhikshuni who acts as a spy, taking information from the Sangha and giving it to a political party or a political organization, commits a Sangha Restoration Offense.

18. A bhikshuni who receives payment from the government, a political party, or a political organization, commits a Sangha Restoration Offense.

19. A bhikshuni who allows laypeople to control her and tell her what to do in order to receive donations loses the qualities of freedom and stability that belong to a nun and commits a Sangha Restoration Offense.

20. A bhikshuni who does not teach the Dharma to the other nuns, does not allow them to visit other places to study the sutras and to have access to clear and effective methods of practice, and as a result, the nuns' study and practice remains incorrect and ineffective, commits a Sangha Restoration Offense.

21. A bhikshuni who has only briefly read or heard about a method of practice belonging to another school of Buddhism or another tradition and has not had a chance to study or put this method into practice, yet publicly speaks or writes an article opposing it, commits a Sangha Restoration Offense.

22. A bhikshuni who says that she does not owe any gratitude to her parents, teachers, friends, or benefactors, commits a Sangha Restoration Offense.

23. A bhikshuni who cuts herself off from the Sangha to set up a hermitage or temple of her own, without the permission of the Sangha, commits a Sangha Restoration Offense.

24. A bhikshuni who builds a hermitage or temple for herself without asking the Sangha about where or in what style she should build it,

builds it larger than is necessary, and builds it in such a way that it causes inconvenience to others or obstructs a road or path that people use, commits a Sangha Restoration Offense.

25. A bhikshuni who, when building a hermitage or temple, becomes involved in a land dispute which leads to a lawsuit, commits a Sangha Restoration Offense.

26. A bhikshuni who turns the practice of chanting the sutra into a way of earning money by quoting a price which should be paid to her for performing a ceremony or a funeral service, commits a Sangha Restoration Offense.

27. A bhikshuni who uses money reserved for the material necessities of the Sangha for construction, while the nuns in the temple do not have enough food, drink, or medicine, commits a Sangha Restoration Offense.

28. A bhikshuni who lives in a careless and disorderly manner causing the laypeople's faith in the Three Jewels to diminish, after having been warned three times without listening deeply and changing her way, commits a Sangha Restoration Offense.

29. A bhikshuni who spends all her time and energy in work, organization, and management with the result that she forgets that the aim of a nun is to practice to liberate herself and other beings from suffering, after having been warned three times without listening deeply and changing her way, commits a Sangha Restoration Offense.

30. A bhikshuni who causes disharmony within the Sangha by her way of speaking and acting, after having been warned three times without listening deeply and changing her way, commits a Sangha Restoration Offense.

31. A bhikshuni who contributes to forming conflicting groups within the Sangha, so that the energy of the practice and harmony of the Sangha goes down, thereby creating the danger of a split in the Sangha, after having been warned three times without listening deeply and changing her way, commits a Sangha Restoration Offense.

32. A bhikshuni who contributes to forming a splinter group within the Sangha, thereby creating the danger of a split in the Sangha, after having been warned three times without listening deeply and changing her way, commits a Sangha Restoration Offense.

33. A bhikshuni who, out of discontentment, using the support and power of the government, causes disharmony in the Sangha, and without the permission of the Sangha cuts herself off from the Sangha and persuades other members of the Sangha to follow her to set up a new community, after having been warned three times without listening deeply and changing her way, commits a Sangha Restoration Offense.

34. A bhikshuni who refuses to listen to the advice and instruction of bhikshus or other bhikshunis regarding her understanding and practice of the Sutra, the Vinaya, and the Shastra, saying that she does not want to be disturbed but left in peace, after having been warned three times without listening deeply and changing her way, commits a Sangha Restoration Offense.

35. A bhikshuni who announces out of anger that she will leave the Sangha, disrobe, or join another religious order, after having been warned three times by another bhikshuni without listening deeply and changing her way, commits a Sangha Restoration Offense.

36. A bhikshuni who gives teachings or leads people in practices which are not in accord with the teachings of transformation, healing, and liberation presented in Buddhism, after having been warned three times without listening deeply and changing her way, commits a Sangha Restoration Offense.

Venerable Bhikshunis, I have finished reciting the Thirty-six Sangha Restoration Offenses. The first twenty-seven precepts are broken as soon as they are committed. The last nine precepts are broken when the bhikshuni has been warned three times to no effect. A bhikshuni who breaks one of these thirty-six precepts and intentionally hides her offense, shall be subject to Dwelling Apart from the Sangha (Manatva) for as long as the time during which she hid the offense. After that she will practice fifteen days of Beginning Anew before the Ceremony of Purifying the Offense.

Now I am asking you: as far as these Thirty-six Sangha Restoration Offenses are concerned, is your precepts' body clear?

[The question is asked three times.]

The Venerable Bhikshunis have remained silent. Therefore we know that in the Sangha everyone's precepts' body is clear. Let us be aware of this, recognize it, and give it our approval. (Bell)

Release and Expression of Regret Offenses (Naihsargika-Payantika)

Venerable Bhikshunis, these are the Forty Release and Expression of Regret Offenses (Naihsargika-Payantika), to be recited once every two weeks.

1. A bhikshuni who keeps in her possession or uses tobacco or any kind of illegal drug which is considered to be a mind-altering substance, commits an offense which involves Release and Expression of Regret.

2. A bhikshuni who keeps and trades in worldly novels, horror stories, or horoscope and fortune-telling materials, commits an offense which involves Release and Expression of Regret.

3. A bhikshuni who keeps for herself or for others toxic cultural items such as worldly films, videotapes, music, or electronic games, commits an offense which involves Release and Expression of Regret.

4. A bhikshuni who keeps a television, video player, karaoke player, electronic games' machine, or any other kind of equipment used for showing worldly films, listening to worldly music, or playing electronic games, commits an offense which involves Release and Expression of Regret.

5. A bhikshuni who has a private e-mail account, except with the permission of the Sangha, commits an offense which involves Release and Expression of Regret.

6. A bhikshuni who keeps in her possession tools which can be used for masturbation, commits an offense which involves Release and Expression of Regret.

7. A bhikshuni who owns her own car or uses expensive, luxurious, or flashy and brightly colored cars or telephones, commits an offense which involves Release and Expression of Regret.

8. A bhikshuni who thinks that money and possessions can guarantee her security and seeks ways to accumulate these things in such a way that they become an obstacle to her path of practice, commits an offense which involves Release and Expression of Regret.

9. A bhikshuni who opens or keeps a bank account for her own use, except when she has the permission of her Sangha to study Buddhism abroad, commits an offense which involves Release and Expression of Regret.

10. A bhikshuni who makes herself the sole manager of the properties of the nunnery or a charitable organization without being designated by the Sangha to do so, commits an offense which involves Release and Expression of Regret.

11. A bhikshuni who uses the nunnery budget or the budget of a charitable organization to give support to her relatives or friends without the consent of other members of the Sangha or the charitable organization, commits an offense which involves Release and Expression of Regret.

12. A bhikshuni who lends money with interest, invests money, buys and sells stocks or shares, invests in land or real estate, or plays the

lottery, commits an offense which involves Release and Expression of Regret.

13. A bhikshuni who wears objects of gold, silver, or precious stones, even though they are a keepsake of a close relation, or has a dental implant or crown made of gold or silver for cosmetic purposes or to display her wealth, commits an offense which involves Release and Expression of Regret.

14. A bhikshuni who uses a rosary made of expensive or brightly colored gems, commits an offense which involves Release and Expression of Regret.

15. A bhikshuni who buys and stores expensive antiques and cherishes them as precious belongings, commits an offense which involves Release and Expression of Regret.

16. A bhikshuni who stores money or jewelry for someone else, commits an offense which involves Release and Expression of Regret.

17. A bhikshuni who keeps in her possession too many books, even if those books are sutras or are connected to Buddhist studies, who is afraid to lend them to others and who refuses to entrust them to the Sangha library for communal use, commits an offense which involves Release and Expression of Regret.

18. A bhikshuni who stores a large amount of cloth and does not hand it over to the community or share it with someone who needs it, commits an offense which involves Release and Expression of Regret.

19. A bhikshuni who has more than three formal robes (the antaravasa, the uttarasangha, and the sanghati), more than three long robes (the ao trang and ao nhat binh), and more than five suits (vat ho) worn under the long robe (not counting work clothes, warm underwear or coats for those living in cold places), and who refuses to hand the excess over to the Sangha for keeping for newly ordained members, commits an offense which involves Release and Expression of Regret.

20. A bhikshuni who wears monastic robes made of translucent, shiny, silky, or colorful material or any kind of material which is sewn with golden thread or glittering beads, commits an offense which involves Release and Expression of Regret.

21. A bhikshuni who makes monastic robes according to a fashionable design or in imitation of clothes worn by wealthy and powerful people, rather than robes that reflect the spirit of monastic simplicity, commits an offense which involves Release and Expression of Regret.

22. A bhikshuni who buys personal luxurious items, commits an offense which involves Release and Expression of Regret.

23. A bhikshuni who keeps and wears expensive or fashionable slippers or shoes with high heels in order to look attractive, commits an offense which involves Release and Expression of Regret.

24. A bhikshuni who uses fashionable or colorful umbrellas, handbags, gloves, or socks, commits an offense which involves Release and Expression of Regret.

25. A bhikshuni who keeps and uses perfume, cosmetic powder, perfumed laundry soap, or any other cosmetics, commits an offense which involves Release and Expression of Regret.

26. A bhikshuni who stores a significant amount of shampoo, laundry soap, toothpaste, towels, toothbrushes, or other toiletries and refuses to share them with the Sangha, commits an offense which involves Release and Expression of Regret.

27. A bhikshuni who is admitted to a hospital for treatment and stays in an expensive, private room with unnecessary luxuries, commits an offense which involves Release and Expression of Regret.

28. A bhikshuni who lies on a luxurious bed, commits an offense which involves Release and Expression of Regret.

29. A bhikshuni who decorates her room in a luxurious way with many comforts like that of people in the world, commits an offense which involves Release and Expression of Regret.

30. A bhikshuni who stores a significant amount of food or drink in her personal storage space and does not bring it out to share with the Sangha, commits an offense which involves Release and Expression of Regret.

31. A bhikshuni who intentionally wears tattered robes in order to arouse pity in a donor, commits an offense which involves Release and Expression of Regret.

32. A bhikshuni who goes to laypeople, whether those people are related to her or not, and collects material objects and funds for her personal

use, commits an offense which involves Release and Expression of Regret.

33. A bhikshuni who uses an offering from a layperson not in accordance with the layperson's wishes and without informing the layperson, so that the layperson suffers or is unhappy and upset, commits an offense which involves Release and Expression of Regret.

34. A bhikshuni who sews, cooks, or manufactures things to sell in order to make money to send home to her family, except when her parents are in ill health and have no other means of financial support, commits an offense which involves Release and Expression of Regret.

35. A bhikshuni who is only interested in sewing, cooking, or manufacturing things to sell, even if it is to create income for the nunnery, and therefore neglects the Sangha practice schedule, commits an offense which involves Release and Expression of Regret.

36. A bhikshuni who raises animals or fowl for entertainment or with the intention to sell them and make money, commits an offense which involves Release and Expression of Regret.

37. A bhikshuni who speaks in such a way so that someone who wants to make a donation to another bhikshuni or to the Sangha changes his or her mind and makes the donation to her instead, commits an offense which involves Release and Expression of Regret.

38. A bhikshuni who keeps items which belong to the whole Sangha for her personal use or gives them to someone else without the permission of the Sangha, commits an offense which involves Release and Expression of Regret.

39. A bhikshuni who uses what belongs to the Sangha in a way that is contrary to the Sangha's wishes, causing discontent or disharmony in the Sangha, commits an offense which involves Release and Expression of Regret.

40. A bhikshuni who uses Sangha resources in a wasteful manner, including money, water, electricity, telephone, car, and so on, commits an offense which involves Release and Expression of Regret.

Venerable Bhikshunis, I have finished reciting the Forty Release and Expression of Regret Offenses. A bhikshuni who transgresses any one of these forty precepts has to come before the Sangha or before three or two other bhikshunis who represent the Sangha in order to release and hand back to the Sangha the money or materials which she has been keeping, and then express her regret and begin anew.

Now I am asking you: as far as these Forty Release and Expression of Regret Offenses are concerned, is your precepts' body clear?

[The question is asked three times.]

The Venerable Bhikshunis have remained silent. Therefore we know that in the Sangha everyone's precepts' body is clear. Let us be aware of this, recognize it, and give it our approval. [Bell]

Expression of Regret Offenses (Payantika)

Venerable Bhikshunis, these are the One Hundred and Forty-two Expression of Regret Offenses (Payantika), to be recited once every two weeks.

1. A bhikshuni who makes an appointment to go outside the nunnery alone with a layman or a monk, commits an Expression of Regret Offense.

2. A bhikshuni who sits alone in a hidden or solitary place with a layman or a monk, commits an Expression of Regret Offense.

3. A bhikshuni who sits alone in a car or on a boat with a layman or a monk, except in the case of an emergency or with the permission of the Sangha, commits an Expression of Regret Offense.

4. A bhikshuni who writes a letter or gives a gift to a layman or a monk in order to show her feeling of affection for him or to win his heart, commits an Expression of Regret Offense.

5. A bhikshuni who accepts gifts from a layman or a monk whose mind is not pure and who has a special affection towards her, commits an Expression of Regret Offense.

6. A bhikshuni who is sick, and refuses to ask for help from her fellow nuns or laywomen, but instead allows one or more monks or laymen to look after her and bring her food, commits an Expression of Regret Offense.

7. A bhikshuni who rents an apartment or a room in a hotel and stays there with monks, even when other bhikshunis are present, except

in special cases when the Sangha has given permission, commits an Expression of Regret Offense.

8. A bhikshuni who goes alone to a monastery where monks are practicing, even if she has been invited in advance, commits an Expression of Regret Offense.

9. A bhikshuni who makes a telephone call to someone of the opposite sex at night, except in an emergency when she has let her fellow practitioners know that she is making this call, commits an Expression of Regret Offense.

10. A bhikshuni who in the course of studying a worldly subject invites the male teacher to come to her place or goes to his place to receive private tutoring, commits an Expression of Regret Offense.

11. A bhikshuni who intentionally seeks a male doctor to take care of her and give her special treatment, except with the permission of the Sangha, commits an Expression of Regret Offense.

12. A bhikshuni who after being reminded by four or more bhikshunis that she is emotionally attached to another person, whether male or female, and who refuses to listen, denies it, tries to negate what they say, or expresses anger, commits an Expression of Regret Offense.

13. A bhikshuni who, because she has a special affection for a monk, often brings other nuns to his room to clean, cook special feasts, and have a party together commits an Expression of Regret Offense.

14. A bhikshuni who brings out all kinds of material items to serve and offer to bhikshus who are well-known, with positions of authority,

in order to please them and give them special treatment and if she treats the nuns in the opposite way so that they are short of food and clothing and suffer hardship, commits an Expression of Regret Offense.

15. A bhikshuni who sleeps on the same bed with another woman, except in special circumstances for which she has informed the other bhikshunis, commits an Expression of Regret Offense.

16. A bhikshuni who sleeps with a dog or a cat commits an Expression of Regret Offense.

17. A bhikshuni who shaves her pubic hair, except in the case of a medical necessity and she has informed another bhikshuni, commits an Expression of Regret Offense.

18. A bhikshuni who is carried away as she touches her breasts or private parts, commits an Expression of Regret Offense.

19. A bhikshuni who masturbates, except in a dream, commits an Expression of Regret Offense.

20. A bhikshuni who intentionally watches animals copulating, commits an Expression of Regret Offense.

21. A bhikshuni who tells stories about sexual relations which she has seen on films, read in books, or heard others tell, commits an Expression of Regret Offense.

22. A bhikshuni who does not wear undergarments when she goes to town or visits a monastery commits an Expression of Regret Offense.

23. A bhikshuni who wears undergarments not approved of for the monastic Sangha, commits an Expression of Regret Offense.

24. A bhikshuni who knows that a woman is presently pregnant, or suckling her child, or has an incurable disease, or is trying to avoid paying debts, or has broken a criminal law, or does not have the agreement of her husband and children to ordain, and still allows that person to receive the Novice Precepts, commits an Expression of Regret Offense.

25. A bhikshuni who knows that a nun is not yet twenty years old, or is twenty years old but has not studied the precepts for two years, or has studied the precepts for two years but has not practiced the six Shikshamana precepts well, or has already received the Bhikshuni Precepts in the past, or has not been accepted by the Sangha as an ordinee, and still allows her to receive the Bhikshuni Precepts, commits an Expression of Regret Offense.[1]

26. A bhikshuni who has not changed her roommate after eight months, except with the permission of the Sangha, commits an Expression of Regret Offense.

27. A bhikshuni who speaks poorly about, jokes about, belittles, or insults a bhikshu, commits an Expression of Regret Offense.

28. A bhikshuni who tries to overpower a bhikshu either through actions or words, commits an Expression of Regret Offense.

---

1 The Shikshamana precepts are precepts received by nuns in preparation for receiving the Bhikshuni precepts. They are traditionally received two years prior to the bhikshuni ordination.

29. A bhikshuni who hits another person in anger or out of resentment, commits an Expression of Regret Offense.

30. A bhikshuni who swears herself to one of the three unwholesome destinies during an argument, such as by saying "If I am lying, I will go to hell," commits an Expression of Regret Offense.

31. A bhikshuni who forces someone to swear an oath, commits an Expression of Regret Offense.

32. A bhikshuni who says what is not true, adds or omits important details, speaks vulgar words to insult others, or speaks words that cause hatred and division, commits an Expression of Regret Offense.

33. A bhikshuni who argues angrily in a loud voice and is gently encouraged by another bhikshuni that she should say no more but return to her breathing or go outside to practice walking meditation in order to guard her mind, and who does not listen and continues to argue in a loud voice, commits an Expression of Regret Offense.

34. A bhikshuni who is offered guidance by a fellow practitioner concerning her shortcomings in the practice, and not only does not receive the guidance with gratitude and respect by joining her palms, but tries to find ways to defend herself, to avoid the subject, or to excuse herself by bringing up the shortcomings of others, commits an Expression of Regret Offense.

35. A bhikshuni who repeatedly speaks in a way that indirectly refers to the wrongdoing done in the past by another bhikshuni, commits an Expression of Regret Offense.

36. A bhikshuni who brings up another bhikshuni's past offense, although the bhikshuni has already been cleared of that offense with a Sangha-karman Procedure, commits an Expression of Regret Offense.

37. A bhikshuni who, during a meal, interrogates or reprimands other nuns in the Sangha, putting them in a difficult situation, commits an Expression of Regret Offense.

38. A bhikshuni who reprimands or punishes other nuns in the Sangha in the presence of laypeople, commits an Expression of Regret Offense.

39. A bhikshuni who threatens or frightens another bhikshuni in such a way that the other becomes fearful and loses her motivation, commits an Expression of Regret Offense.

40. A bhikshuni who is requested to come and resolve a conflict with someone and continuously finds ways to avoid being present to make the reconciliation, commits an Expression of Regret Offense.

41. A bhikshuni who refuses to accept someone else's apology, commits an Expression of Regret Offense.

42. A bhikshuni who, out of anger, throws the belongings of another person, commits an Expression of Regret Offense.

43. A bhikshuni who allows her anger to continue up to seven days and still has no intention to practice reconciliation and Beginning Anew, commits an Expression of Regret Offense.

44. A bhikshuni who, out of anger or jealousy, accuses another bhikshuni of committing a Sangha Restoration Offense, which has no

basis in reality, in order to destroy her reputation, commits an Expression of Regret Offense.

45. A bhikshuni who, out of hatred or discrimination, repeatedly and aggressively disputes in words or writing with other ideologies or religious faiths instead of devoting herself to her studies and practice, commits an Expression of Regret Offense.

46. A bhikshuni who because of resentment with her fellow practitioners does not seek help from the Sangha to find ways of reconciliation and instead leaves the community to go somewhere else or goes to stay with her family for a while and then comes back again, commits an Expression of Regret Offense.

47. A bhikshuni who does not practice to restore communication with her fellow practitioners but only complains to laypeople about difficulties and conflicts in the Sangha, commits an Expression of Regret Offense.

48. A bhikshuni who does not use loving speech and deep listening to resolve the difficulties and disputes that have arisen between her and another nun, but instead only goes to complain to and seek an ally in one person after another, commits an Expression of Regret Offense.

49. A bhikshuni who, upon hearing another nun complain about her difficulties with a third nun, makes no effort to bring about reconciliation between them, and instead allies herself with the nun who has complained to her in order to oppose the third nun, commits an Expression of Regret Offense.

50. A bhikshuni who goes to another nunnery and talks about the short-comings and weaknesses of her former nunnery in a complaining and reproachful way, commits an Expression of Regret Offense.

51. A bhikshuni who claims to be up to date with the modern way of life and looks down disrespectfully on her teacher for being out-dated and out of touch, commits an Expression of Regret Offense.

52. A bhikshuni who knows that the Sangha is about to meet to perform a Sanghakarman Procedure, and who finds ways not to be present or pretends to be unwell and does not ask to be represented, commits an Expression of Regret Offense.

53. A bhikshuni who has already performed a Sanghakarman Procedure with the Sangha but is still annoyed and displeased about the meeting and tells someone else that she is against the Sanghakarman Procedure that has been realized, commits an Expression of Regret Offense.

54. A bhikshuni who has formally asked someone to represent her at a Sangha meeting and afterwards, feeling regret, looks for ways to deny the resolution that has been realized by Sanghakarman Procedure, commits an Expression of Regret Offense.

55. A bhikshuni who does not put into effect, or encourages someone else to not put into effect a resolution that has been taken by the Sangha under Sanghakarman Procedure, commits an Expression of Regret Offense.

56. A bhikshuni who persists in defending another bhikshuni whom the Sangha has asked to practice Dwelling Apart from the Sangha

(Manatva), after being warned three times without listening deeply and changing her way, commits an Expression of Regret Offense.

57. A bhikshuni who talks about the faults of another nun when that nun is not present, except in the case of the practice of Shining Light, commits an Expression of Regret Offense.

58. A bhikshuni who promises to give a robe or other item to another person but later out of anger takes back her word, or if she has already given the item asks for it back, commits an Expression of Regret Offense.

59. A bhikshuni who hides the belongings of another person, causing that person to be anxious and fearful, commits an Expression of Regret Offense.

60. A bhikshuni who sees that a fellow nun is sick and does not ask about her condition and look after her or find someone else to look after her, commits an Expression of Regret Offense.

61. A bhikshuni who has been assigned by the Sangha to distribute items among Sangha members, but out of favoritism gives more to some nuns and less to others, or refuses to give anything to a nun with whom she does not get along well, commits an Expression of Regret Offense.

62. A bhikshuni who closes her eyes before suffering within herself and in the world and only takes comfort in laypeople's offerings, forgetting that the aim of the practice is to find ways to transform suffering into peace and joy, after having been warned by three other

bhikshunis without listening deeply and changing her way, commits an Expression of Regret Offense.

63. A bhikshuni who sees that her fellow nun is about to commit an offense and says nothing to dissuade her against it or to let other bhikshunis know so they can dissuade her against it, commits an Expression of Regret Offense.

64. A bhikshuni who knows that another bhikshuni is deliberately hiding her offenses but is not willing to persuade that bhikshuni to admit her faults, express regret, and begin anew before the Sangha, nor does she report the matter to the Sangha so that they can find ways to help the offending bhikshuni recover the purity of her practice, commits an Expression of Regret Offense.

65. A bhikshuni who pretends to be a pregnant woman, a disabled person, or a beggar as a joke or in mockery, commits an Expression of Regret Offense.

66. A bhikshuni who is narrow-minded, attached to her views, and maintains that the knowledge she presently possesses is absolute and unchanging, refusing to be open to and receiving the viewpoints of others, after having been warned by three other bhikshunis and still refusing to alter her attitude, commits an Expression of Regret Offense.

67. A bhikshuni who uses authority, bribery, threat, propaganda, or indoctrination to force others, including children, to adopt her view, who does not respect the right of others to be different or their free-

dom to choose what to believe and how to decide, after having been warned by three other bhikshunis and still refusing to alter her attitude, commits an Expression of Regret Offense.

68. A bhikshuni who has relatives who are monks or nuns and uses her authority to protect them when they act wrongly or seeks ways to give them priority or privilege, commits an Expression of Regret Offense.

69. A bhikshuni who relies on her sphere of influence due to the office she holds in the Sangha in order to overpower another bhikshuni who is her senior in years of ordination, commits an Expression of Regret Offense.

70. A bhikshuni who uses her authority to force another bhikshuni to take her side in opposing a proposal which is about to be realized by a Sanghakarman Procedure, commits an Expression of Regret Offense.

71. A bhikshuni who is attached to her title or position of seniority in the Sangha, and becomes angry or annoyed when someone does not address her according to her position or tells that person that they should correct their way of addressing her, commits an Expression of Regret Offense.

72. A bhikshuni who does not take care of enriching the quality of her practice as a nun but competes for or entices the disciples of another teacher, so that there is animosity between the bhikshuni and the other teacher, commits an Expression of Regret Offense.

73. A bhikshuni who only gives special treatment to her own disciples and fails to care for other students who come to ask her for mentorship, commits an Expression of Regret Offense.

74. A bhikshuni who encourages another nun to take her side so that she can have more power to overtake fellow practitioners, commits an Expression of Regret Offense.

75. A bhikshuni who encourages another nun to leave her teacher and root temple in order to set up her own hermitage or go to another nunnery, commits an Expression of Regret Offense.

76. A bhikshuni who speaks in a sweet and exaggerating way to win someone's heart or complains and cries to arouse others' sympathy for herself, commits an Expression of Regret Offense.

77. A bhikshuni who spreads news that she does not know to be certain or criticizes and condemns things of which she is not sure, in order to gain money, material benefits, or admiration for herself, commits an Expression of Regret Offense.

78. A bhikshuni who, after having received donations from a layperson, defends that layperson and oppresses other nuns or monks, commits an Expression of Regret Offense.

79. A bhikshuni who accepts disciples not with the purpose to teach and nurture them on the path of practice but only to serve her own reputation or her personal work, commits an Expression of Regret Offense.

80. A bhikshuni who forces the nuns to work hard sewing or manufacturing things to sell in order to increase the income of the nunnery and thus does not allow them enough time for their studies and practice, commits an Expression of Regret Offense.

81. A bhikshuni who makes hints in many ways in order to receive donations, commits an Expression of Regret Offense.

82. A bhikshuni who pretends that she has a serious illness in order to be cared for by donors or to receive donations, commits an Expression of Regret Offense.

83. A bhikshuni who takes advantage of charitable organizations associated with the nunnery in order to gather additional possessions for herself or her nunnery, commits an Expression of Regret Offense.

84. A bhikshuni who criticizes and looks down on an offering made by a donor to the Sangha, commits an Expression of Regret Offense.

85. A bhikshuni who accepts offerings from laypeople but does not truly practice to transform herself and says that it is the duty of laypeople to bring her offerings, commits an Expression of Regret Offense.

86. A bhikshuni who goes to a monks' monastery to complain about her lack of material resources in order to receive an offering, commits an Expression of Regret Offense.

87. A bhikshuni who only meets with people who are rich or intellectual, and out of discrimination does not show concern for those who are poor or uneducated, commits an Expression of Regret Offense.

88. A bhikshuni who borrows what belongs to another and does not return it in a timely manner, thus causing the other annoyance and displeasure, commits an Expression of Regret Offense.

89. A bhikshuni who steals money or belongings of another person, tells someone else to steal them, or sees someone stealing them without finding ways to prevent it, commits an Expression of Regret Offense.

90. A bhikshuni who breaks the promise she has made to a layperson and thus makes that person angry and critical of the monastic Sangha, commits an Expression of Regret Offense.

91. A bhikshuni who avoids heavy work and looks for light work, except in the case of illness or if she is weak and has poor health, commits an Expression of Regret Offense.

92. A bhikshuni who assesses the value of someone by the work she does, forgetting that the quality of a nun's practice is more important than the amount of work she accomplishes, commits an Expression of Regret Offense.

93. A bhikshuni who is not aware that the the responsibility of a monastic is to offer concrete practices which help people transform their suffering, but instead focuses all her energy on charitable works, forcing the Sangha to work so hard that they neglect their program of spiritual studies and practice, commits an Expression of Regret Offense.

94. A bhikshuni who accepts hired work to earn some money for herself, not recognizing that her nunnery already has the resources to

support her material needs and spiritual studies and practice, commits an Expression of Regret Offense.

95. A bhikshuni who tells people's fortunes (by reading palms, astrology, or other means) or burns paper money for the deceased in order to earn some money, commits an Expression of Regret Offense.

96. A bhikshuni who eats a non-vegetarian meal, even though she excuses herself by saying that she lacks nutrition, commits an Expression of Regret Offense.

97. A bhikshuni who, out of greed, eats and drinks without moderation, commits an Expression of Regret Offense.

98. A bhikshuni who neglects the practice activities of the Sangha in order to produce luxurious and fancy dishes using expensive ingredients, without considering that so many people in the world are suffering from hunger and forgetting that she has committed herself to live the simple life of a nun, commits an Expression of Regret Offense.

99. A bhikshuni who eats apart from the Sangha and eats in her room, except when she is sick or is unable to eat with the Sangha due to Sangha service, commits an Expression of Regret Offense.

100. A bhikshuni who drinks beer, wine, or liquor of any kind, or takes any other substance that causes inebriation, except for medicinal use with the permission of the Bhikshuni Sangha, commits an Expression of Regret Offense.

101. A bhikshuni who enters a bar or a dimly lit coffee shop to have a drink or to sit and watch people come and go, commits an Expression of Regret Offense.

102. A bhikshuni who goes to a layperson's house or a restaurant to attend a birthday party, an engagement reception, or a wedding reception, commits an Expression of Regret Offense.

103. A bhikshuni who celebrates her birthday in a layperson's house or a restaurant, commits an Expression of Regret Offense.

104. A bhikshuni who goes as a spectator to sports games, cinema, or worldly concerts, commits an Expression of Regret Offense.

105. A bhikshuni who rents and watches videos, or reads books and magazines which have a toxic effect, watering the seeds of sexual desire, fear, violence, sentimental weakness, and depression, commits an Expression of Regret Offense.

106. A bhikshuni who watches television programs which have a toxic effect, watering the seeds of sexual desire, fear, violence, sentimental weakness, and depression, commits an Expression of Regret Offense.

107. A bhikshuni who goes on to the Internet alone, without another nun next to her as a protection against getting lost in toxic Websites, commits an Expression of Regret Offense.

108. A bhikshuni who consumes images or sounds which excite sexual desire from the Internet or the telephone, commits an Expression of Regret Offense.

109. A bhikshuni who listens to or performs songs or music that is sad, sentimental, romantic, or exciting (such as rock music), commits an Expression of Regret Offense.

110. A bhikshuni who plays electronic games, including those on a mobile phone or a computer, commits an Expression of Regret Offense.

111. A bhikshuni who gambles or bets on horse races, car races, and other sports commits an Expression of Regret Offense.

112. A bhikshuni who drives in a careless and dangerous manner, speeding, swerving between cars, recklessly passing other cars, accelerating too quickly, or racing with another car, commits an Expression of Regret Offense.

113. A bhikshuni who marches down the street clapping her hands, shouting, waving a flag, or throwing flowers to show support for a sports team, commits an Expression of Regret Offense.

114. A bhikshuni who goes to watch military drills or preparations for battle, people fighting or arguing with each other, a martial art performance, or a magic show, commits an Expression of Regret Offense.

115. A bhikshuni who goes to watch animals fighting or provokes animals to fight with each other, commits an Expression of Regret Offense.

116. A bhikshuni who abuses animals or takes their bones, horns, or skin to make artwork or decorations, commits an Expression of Regret Offense.

117. A bhikshuni who does not cultivate compassion and learn ways to protect the lives of animals, who kills an animal herself, gives consent for an animal to be killed, or does not prevent someone else from killing an animal, commits an Expression of Regret Offense.

118. A bhikshuni who cooks meat for dogs or cats, commits an Expression of Regret Offense.

119. A bhikshuni who pollutes the environment, by burning and destroying forests or by using toxic chemicals, for example, commits an Expression of Regret Offense.

120. A bhikshuni who intentionally allows her hair to grow long, commits an Expression of Regret Offense.

121. A bhikshuni who goes to a beauty clinic in order to improve her appearance, commits an Expression of Regret Offense.

122. A bhikshuni who is not aware that the true beauty of a nun is found in her solidity and freedom, and instead spends too much time and care in dressing herself in order to create an outer show of attractiveness, commits an Expression of Regret Offense.

123. A bhikshuni who when going into a town, village, or market wears lay clothing or a wig, commits an Expression of Regret Offense.

124. A bhikshuni who separates herself from the Sangha and rents her own lodgings, commits an Expression of Regret Offense.

125. A bhikshuni who sleeps overnight in a layperson's house, even for Sangha service, and at least one other female practitioner does not accompany her, except in special circumstances with the permission of the Sangha, commits an Expression of Regret Offense.

126. A bhikshuni who stays longer than one week in a layperson's house, except with the permission of the Sangha, commits an Expression of Regret Offense.

127. A bhikshuni who goes outside the nunnery alone or separates from the person with whom she has left the nunnery, unaware of the danger that could threaten her practice of the precepts, commits an Expression of Regret Offense.

128. A bhikshuni who commits herself to a special relationship with a layperson by asking that person to be her father, mother, brother, sister, son, daughter, or grandchild, commits an Expression of Regret Offense.

129. A bhikshuni who undertakes a course of study with the purpose of being awarded a bachelor's degree, master's degree, or doctorate in engineering, medicine, pharmacy, or other worldly subjects, except in the case that the course is in Buddhist studies, commits an Expression of Regret Offense.

130. A bhikshuni who spends all her time studying worldly subjects, therefore neglecting to learn spiritual teachings and practice, commits an Expression of Regret Offense.

131. A bhikshuni who immerses herself in and is carried away by her work and as a result fails to maintain good relationships between

herself and other members of the Sangha, commits an Expression of Regret Offense.

132. A bhikshuni who leaves her mentor before she has completed her fifth Rains' Retreat, or even after this time if her practice is still weak, commits an Expression of Regret Offense.

133. A bhikshuni who does not complete the three-month Rains' Retreat once a year, commits an Expression of Regret Offense.

134. A bhikshuni who goes outside the officially declared boundaries of the Rains' Retreat for an equal or greater number of days than she is within these boudaries, even if her reason for going outside is to teach, study, or do charitable work, commits an Expression of Regret Offense.

135. A bhikshuni who does not go to the bhikshus to request teachings at least once in three months, commits an Expression of Regret Offense.

136. A bhikshuni who at the end of the Rains' Retreat refuses to go to the Bhikshu Sangha to express what she has seen, heard, or has doubts about concerning her own practice in order to receive Shining Light from the bhikshus, commits an Expression of Regret Offense.

137. A bhikshuni who passes the three-month Rains' Retreat in a place where there is no Bhikshu Sangha, commits an Expression of Regret Offense.

138. A bhikshuni who transmits the Bhikshuni Precepts without yet completing twelve Rains' Retreats, commits an Expression of Regret Offense.

139. A bhikshuni who has not mastered the Vinaya and who performs a Sanghakarman Procedure or makes the affirmation of an offense in a way which is not in accordance with the Vinaya, thus causing the Sangha to lose its peace, joy, and harmony, commits an Expression of Regret Offense.

140. A bhikshuni who complains about the precepts and fine manners, saying that the articles presented are bothersome, too complicated, too detailed, not truly necessary, and that they take away one's freedom, commits an Expression of Regret Offense.

141. A bhikshuni who does not recite the Pratimoksha with the Sangha at least once in three months, unless she has a long-lasting and serious illness, commits an Expression of Regret Offense.

142. A bhikshuni who has not yet begun to study the Classical Pratimoksha in parallel with the Revised Pratimoksha after one year of receiving the full ordination, commits an Expression of Regret Offense.

Venerable Bhikshunis, I have finished reciting the One Hundred and Forty-two Expression of Regret Offenses. A bhikshuni who transgresses any one of these one hundred and forty-two precepts has to express her regret and begin anew before three or two bhikshunis in order to make her precepts' body clear.

Now I am asking you, as far as these One Hundred and Forty-two Expression of Regret Offenses are concerned, is your precepts' body clear?

[The question is asked three times.]

The Venerable Bhikshunis have remained silent. Therefore we know that in the Sangha everyone's precepts' body is clear. Let us be aware of this, recognize it, and give it our approval. [Bell]

Fine Manners Offenses (Shaiksha)

Venerable Bhikshunis, these are the One Hundred and Fifteen Fine Manners Offenses (Shaiksha), to be recited once every two weeks.

1. A bhikshuni, while walking, should not talk, laugh, joke, whistle, sing, or shout to someone far off.

2. A bhikshuni, while walking, should not chew her food, use a toothpick, or talk on the telephone.

3. A bhikshuni, while walking, should not join her palms in greeting, snap her fingers, swing her arms, sway her body, move her arms and legs as if she were dancing, skip, or turn her face up to the sky.

4. A bhikshuni, while walking, should not walk in haste, but her bearing should emanate solidity and freedom.

5. A bhikshuni, while walking, should not be putting on clothes or adjusting her robe.

6. A bhikshuni, while walking, should not drag or stamp her feet, nor take very long strides.

7. A bhikshuni should not interrupt someone who is speaking.

8. A bhikshuni should not speak so loudly that her voice drowns the voices of others.

9. A bhikshuni should not talk back and forth in a flirtatious way.

10. A bhikshuni, while speaking, should not point her finger towards the other person's face.

11. A bhikshuni should practice to speak softly and slowly, not talking too fast and swallowing her words.

12. A bhikshuni, while speaking, should not intentionally leave her sentence unfinished.

13. A bhikshuni should not engage in a casual conversation about the relationship of a couple, contraception, or giving birth.

14. A bhikshuni should not speak in such a way to probe into someone's personal life to discover her faults, nor should she speak with a sharp, sarcastic, or rough voice.

15. A bhikshuni should not tell ghost or horror stories that water the seeds of fear in another person.

16. A bhikshuni, while speaking, should not glance around or blink flirtatiously.

17. A bhikshuni should not imitate someone else's way of speaking or manner in order to make fun of that person.

18. A bhikshuni should not laugh too loudly or open her mouth too wide.

19. A bhikshuni should not put out her tongue and lick her lips.

20. A bhikshuni should not yawn or pick her teeth without covering her mouth.

21. A bhikshuni should not squat.

22. A bhikshuni should sit solidly and at ease with her back upright, without shaking her legs, or swinging or tapping her feet.

23. A bhikshuni should not sit in a place where people are drinking alcohol, eating meat, gambling, using abusive language, disrespectfully teasing each other, or speaking badly about others.

24. A bhikshuni should practice lying on her right side to go to sleep as this is the most peaceful and healthy position.

25. A bhikshuni should not read or chant the sutras when lying down, except when she is sick.

26. A bhikshuni should not lie down in a place where people pass by, except in special cases.

27. A bhikshuni should stand with a relaxed and upright posture, not leaning against a wall, even while waiting in a line.

28. A bhikshuni should not stand with her hands on her hips, nor should she hold her hands behind her back.

29. A bhikshuni should not choose only the best tasting food for herself.

30. A bhikshuni, while eating, should not chew and swallow her food in a rush, but should chew each mouthful slowly about thirty times before swallowing.

31. A bhikshuni should not talk during a meal.

32. A bhikshuni should not chew and slurp loudly.

33. A bhikshuni should not lick the food from her bowl or plate with her tongue and should not open her mouth too wide when putting food into it.

34. A bhikshuni should not put down her empty bowl when those who have been ordained longer than her are still eating in a formal meal.

35. A bhikshuni should not leave leftover food when she is finished eating.

36. A bhikshuni should not stand up in the middle of a meal, nor stand up as soon as she has finished eating, before the sound of the bell.

37. A bhikshuni should eat lightly in the evening so that she feels light in body and avoids wasting time cooking.

38. A bhikshuni should not buy luxurious and expensive food items, such as tea, sweets and so on, except in special cases.

39. A bhikshuni should care for her alms bowl with respect and should not use more than one alms bowl.

40. A bhikshuni should not make noise with her spoon or chopsticks against her alms bowl.

41. A bhikshuni should always be neatly dressed wearing her long robe when she goes outside the nunnery.

42. A bhikshuni should not dress untidily or wear dirty robes.

43. A bhikshuni should wear an undershirt which goes below her waist.

44. A bhikshuni should be properly dressed so that it is not possible to see the undergarments she is wearing.

45. A bhikshuni should not use tampons worn internally when menstruating.

46. A bhikshuni should completely wrap used sanitary napkins before placing them in the rubbish bin.

47. A bhikshuni should dry her undergarments in the designated place.

48. A bhikshuni should not talk or joke as she is putting on her clothes.

49. A bhikshuni should not let her fingernails grow long or trim them so that they are tapered.

50. A bhikshuni should not trim, pluck, or darken her eyebrows.

51. A bhikshuni should bathe regularly enough so that her body does not have odors.

52. A bhikshuni should exercise regularly so that she remains strong and healthy.

53. A bhikshuni should learn the way to conserve the three energies (sexual, breath, and spirit.)

54. A bhikshuni should clean her teeth after every meal.

55. A bhikshuni, while cleaning her teeth, should not walk back and forth, talk, laugh, or joke.

56. A bhikshuni who has a nightmare should not allow herself to go back to sleep immediately, but should sit up and massage so that the blood circulates evenly, or practice walking meditation outside for ten minutes before going back to sleep.

57. A bhikshuni should not join her palms to bow in a mechanical way, without mindfulness.

58. A bhikshuni should bow when receiving something offered by someone, joining her palms like a lotus bud.

59. A bhikshuni should practice looking straight ahead with calm and ease, not glancing nervously from side to side.

60. A bhikshuni should practice looking deeply while touching the earth, not just prostrating mechanically, and while in this position her four limbs and forehead should touch the ground.

61. A bhikshuni should not urinate or defecate near a stupa or shrine, in a place which is not shielded from view, in a vegetable plot, or in a flowing body of water.

62. A bhikshuni should knock slowly three times before entering someone else's room.

63. A bhikshuni should not leave her shoes or slippers untidily, but should leave them neatly in a straight line.

64. A bhikshuni should neatly arrange and tidy everything when she is finished using it.

65. A bhikshuni should not leave her clothes soaking for a long period of time without washing and drying them so that they do not disintegrate in a short time.

66. A bhikshuni should not reserve the best seat for herself in the Dharma Hall.

67. A bhikshuni should rearrange her cushion and mat tidily when she stands up after the sitting meditation session, kneeling down and using her hands to straighten the cushion and mat, not using her feet.

68. A bhikshuni, before inviting the sound of any bell, should breathe in and out mindfully three times and recite the gatha for inviting the bell.

69. A bhikshuni, upon hearing the sound of the bell, should stop all thinking, speech, and movement, practicing mindful breathing.

70. A bhikshuni should respect the schedule of the Sangha by being present and arriving on time for all activities so that she may be a model for her fellow practitioners.

71. A bhikshuni should not arrive in the Dharma Hall after the teacher has arrived and should not leave in the middle of the Dharma talk.

72. A bhikshuni, while listening to a recording of a Dharma talk, should sit upright, listening with all her attention and respect as she would in the Dharma Hall.

73. A bhikshuni, when hearing the telephone ring, should give rise to mindfulness, returning to her breathing for at least three breaths before picking up the telephone.

74. A bhikshuni, while talking on the telephone, should sit in an upright posture, not speaking too loudly, or teasing or joking.

75. A bhikshuni should only use the telephone for necessary conversations, using loving speech.

76. A bhikshuni, upon hearing the person on the other end of the line making unnecessary conversation, should find a way to politely excuse herself before hanging up the telephone.

77. A bhikshuni should not use a portable telephone during sitting or walking meditation, sutra chanting, Sangha meetings, or study classes.

78. A bhikshuni, while bathing, should not sing, recite the sutras, talk loudly, tease, or joke.

79. A bhikshuni, while cooking or working, should practice mindfulness just as she does during sitting meditation or other Dharma practices and should move around in a calm manner, without rushing.

80. A bhikshuni who is given a special task by the Sangha should not use it in such a way to give her authority or consider that her work is more important than others' work. She should be aware that all kinds of work done to serve the Sangha are equally important.

81. A bhikshuni who is given a special task should not take advantage of it to unnecessarily excuse herself from activities of the Sangha.

82. A bhikshuni, when receiving a task from the Sangha, no matter how important it is, should always do it with ease and freedom.

83. A bhikshuni should not take on more work beyond her capability or state of health. She should not be afraid of inconveniencing others and accept more work, which will then make her anxious, tired, and dispirited.

84. A bhikshuni who is studying teachings of a profound, metaphysical, and mystical nature, should constantly ask herself how she may apply these teachings in her daily life to transform her suffering and realize liberation.

85. A bhikshuni should not read books and sutras without applying the basic and essential practices of Buddhism in order to transform her afflictions and habit energies.

86. A bhikshuni, in addition to reading books on Buddhism, should also read books on the history of civilizations of the world, general history and teachings of other religious faiths, applied psychology, and the most recent scientific discoveries. These areas of knowledge can help her to understand and share the teachings with people in a way that is appropriate to their situation.

87. A bhikshuni should only ask to leave her Sangha and practice elsewhere when she sees that there are not enough conditions for her progress in her present situation. She should choose to go to a nunnery where there is harmony and happiness in the Sangha.

88. A bhikshuni who is overly sensitive, should not react inappropriately to situations, for example, not speaking with another person without letting that person know that she is unhappy or upset.

89. A bhikshuni, when she sees anger arising in herself, should not say or do anything, but practice mindful breathing, not continuing to listen and give attention to the person whom she thinks is the cause of her anger. If necessary she may go outside to practice walking meditation to look deeply, recognizing that the main cause of her anger is the seed of anger within herself.

90. A bhikshuni should offer her insights to the Sangha and accept the decisions and solutions offered by the Sangha, aware that the collective insight of the Sangha, when it contains and harmonizes all the insights of the members of the Sangha, surpasses that of any one individual.

91. A bhikshuni who encounters difficulties in her practice or her work, should share them with fellow practitioners, not hiding them in her heart, so that she can be supported and embraced by the Sangha.

92. A bhikshuni should have another nun as a second body to look after and support, just as she herself is the second body of another nun who supports and looks after her.

93. A bhikshuni should not go outside the nunnery at night, except in an emergency, and if she does have to go outside, she should let the Sangha know and another nun should accompany her.

94. A bhikshuni should bring one formal robe with her if she has to be away from her nunnery overnight.

95. A bhikshuni, while driving, should not make unnecessary conversation, tease, joke, talk on the telephone, read the map or drive her

vehicle alongside another vehicle in order to hold a conversation with the driver of the other vehicle.

96. A bhikshuni, when she drives, should take her driver's license and the official papers of the car she is driving with her.

97. A bhikshuni should wear her seat belt, and when getting into a car or onto a motorbike, should arrange her robes so that they do not hang outside the car or get stuck in the wheel of the motorbike.

98. A bhikshuni should not drive faster than the official speed limit.

99. A bhikshuni should not honk the horn of her car in irritation at another vehicle.

100. A bhikshuni who is driving on a long trip and begins to feel sleepy or tired, should ask someone else to drive. If there is no one to replace her, she should stop the car and rest until she feels refreshed and awake, aware that the lives of the passengers in the car she is driving depend on her careful attention.

101. A bhikshuni, when going shopping, should not express criticism of the merchandise through words or a physical gesture. She should not criticize the price for being too high or return goods once she has already bought them, unless there is a store policy for returns or she has a previous agreement with the seller.

102. A bhikshuni should not buy goods on credit or engage in hard bargaining.

103. A bhikshuni who has promised she will buy goods from one vendor should keep her promise even if she sees the same goods being sold at a cheaper price elsewhere.

104. A bhikshuni should not go into a shop or area where toxic books, magazines, and posters are displayed or sold.

105. A bhikshuni should not tease and joke with a vendor.

106. A bhikshuni who, going outside of the nunnery, meets a high monk or nun of her own tradition should stop, join her palms, and exchange greetings with him or her. If she meets a monk or nun of a different tradition, she should do the same.

107. A bhikshuni should not loiter in a layperson's house or in the town to engage in idle conversation or to eat snacks.

108. A bhikshuni should always have her head covered with the head-scarf when she visits a monastery, goes to town, or to a festival.

109. A bhikshuni should not visit her family more frequently than the Sangha's guidelines allow. She may regularly write home to her family, sharing her happiness and spiritual practice so that her family's happiness and faith in the practice will increase.

110. A bhikshuni should not tell her family about the difficulties she encounters in her life as a nun in such a way that they become concerned and anxious about her.

111. A bhikshuni, when helping to resolve difficult situations in her family, should use her energy of mindfulness and share the practices of deep listening and loving speech.

112. A bhikshuni, when visiting her family, should not keep asking for one thing after another, and when her family gives her something, she should share it with the Sangha.

113. A bhikshuni, when receiving and talking with visiting laypeople in the nunnery, should refrain from taking part in conversations about worldly matters containing blame, criticism, or discrimination. Rather she should listen deeply to the lay practitioner's suffering, and using her own experience in the practice, should offer concrete practices which will help the lay practitioner transform herself as well as the situation in her family and society.

114. A bhikshuni, when receiving and talking with visiting laypeople in the nunnery, should not listen to tales about the shortcomings of other practice centers or monks or nuns from other temples.

115. A bhikshuni should not try to find ways to be in close contact only with people who are powerful, wealthy, or famous.

Venerable Bhikshunis, I have finished reciting the One Hundred and Fifteen Fine Manners Offenses (Shaiksha). A bhikshuni who transgresses any one of these one hundred and fifteen offenses should know that her practice is still weak. She should give rise to a feeling of remorse and promise to her mentor that she will practice more solidly.

Now I am asking you: as far as these One Hundred and Fifteen Fine Manners Offenses are concerned, have you practiced with stability?

[The question is asked three times.]

The Venerable Bhikshunis have remained silent. Therefore we know that in the Sangha the fine manners have been practiced with stability. Let us be aware of this, recognize it, and give it our approval. [Bell]

Seven Ways of Putting an End to Disputes

Venerable Bhikshunis, these are the Seven Ways of Putting an End to Disputes (Sapta dhikarana-shamatha-dharma), to be recited once every two weeks.

1. If a meeting of the Sangha is needed with the presence of those who are involved in the dispute so that they can talk about the injustice and suffering they have experienced, and during this meeting the Sangha can practice deep and compassionate listening in order to relieve the suffering of both sides, then let the Sangha call such a meeting to resolve the dispute.

2. If a meeting is needed to encourage those involved in the dispute to recall and tell what they have seen, heard, and thought about the dispute in the spirit of deep listening and loving speech, then let such a meeting be called to resolve the dispute.

3. If a meeting is needed to affirm that a person involved in the dispute was going through a mental crisis or illness at the time of the dispute and did not know that she was causing difficulties and making others suffer, and now that the crisis is over she still cannot remember well what happened, then let such a meeting be called to resolve the dispute.

4. If a meeting is needed to give those who are involved in the dispute an opportunity to recognize and acknowledge their own unskillfulness and lack of mindfulness, wherein one person first expresses her unskilfulness, lack of mindfulness, and regrets using loving speech,

and then the other person(s) will be encouraged to do the same, helping to de-escalate the conflict, then let such a meeting be called to resolve the dispute.

5. If a meeting is needed to appoint a committee to investigate and study the causes and nature of the dispute, and after investigating this committee should present a report to the Sangha so that they can resolve the dispute, then let such a meeting be called to resolve the dispute.

6. If a meeting is needed to resolve the dispute by means of a majority vote, since the dispute has gone on so long unresolved, and after the decision by majority is made no one can bring the matter up again, then let such a meeting be called to resolve the dispute.

7. If a meeting in the presence of the most respected elders of the community is needed to resolve a dispute and in this meeting the elders will declare a general amnesty, encouraging everyone to use their compassion to put an end to resentment, like laying straw on the mud, then let such a meeting be called to resolve the dispute.

Venerable Bhikshunis, I have finished reciting the Seven Ways of Putting an End to Disputes.

Now I am asking you: has everyone in the Sangha studied, practiced, and observed these Seven Ways of Putting an End to Disputes?

[The question is asked three times.]

The Venerable Bhikshunis have remained silent. Therefore we know that in the Sangha everyone has studied, practiced and observed these Seven Ways of Putting an End to Disputes. Let us be aware of this, recognize it, and give it our approval. [Bell]

CONCLUSION

Venerable Bhikshunis, I have finished reciting the 348 Bhikshuni Precepts, including the Eight Degradation Offenses, the Thirty-six Sangha Restoration Offenses, the Forty Release and Expression of Regret Offenses, the One Hundred and Forty-two Expression of Regret Offenses, the One Hundred and Fifteen Fine Manners Offenses, and the Seven Ways of Putting an End to Disputes. I wish to thank the Venerable Bhikshunis for helping me to recite the precepts serenely.

[In the unusual circumstance that we cannot recite all 348 of the Bhikshuni Precepts we can use the following conclusion:

Venerable Bhikshunis, I have finished reciting the Bhikshuni Precepts, including the Eight Degradation Offenses and _____ (list the precepts which were recited today). You should read and study for yourself the remaining precepts so that your practice of the precepts can deepen and grow more extensive day by day. I wish to thank the Venerable Bhikshunis for helping me to recite the precepts serenely.]

Venerable Bhikshunis, now I will recite the Four Objects of Refuge and the Four Ways of Meeting with Certain Situations, the essential practices that have been devised by the Buddha and transmitted to us from the Original Sangha of the Buddha. Please listen wholeheartedly and put them into practice.

Here are the Four Objects of Refuge:

1. A bhikshuni takes refuge in her sanghati robe as a bird relies on its wings.

2. A bhikshuni takes refuge in her begging bowl in order to practice humility, to have the opportunity to be in contact with laypeople and to help them realize awakening.

3. A bhikshuni takes refuge in the foot of a tree, a hermitage, or a monastery as her dwelling place, and never leaves her Sangha.

4. A bhikshuni takes refuge in plants, herbs and simple, wholesome foods in order to cure disease.

Here are the Four Ways of Meeting with Certain Situations:

1. A bhikshuni who is insulted by someone, shall not insult that person in return.

2. A bhikshuni whom someone is angry with, shall not be angry with that person in return.

3. A bhikshuni who is belittled by someone, shall not belittle that person in return.

4. A bhikshuni who is beaten by someone, shall not beat that person in return. [Bell]

Inspiring Verses by the Seven Buddhas

Buddha Vipashyin has taught:
Inclusiveness is the first practice.
Nirvana is the final aim.
To make others suffer
is not the practice of a monastic.

Buddha Shikhin has taught:
Someone whose eyes are bright
avoids perilous paths.
The wise ones in the world
do not fall into realms of suffering.

Buddha Vishvabhu has taught:
Not denigrating or envious of others,
practicing and observing the precepts,
eating and drinking with moderation,
diligently dwelling in peace,
this is what the Buddha teaches.

Buddha Krakucchanda has taught:
Just as when the bee visits the flower,
it does not destroy its fragrance and beauty,
but only removes the sweet nectar,
a bhikshuni when going out into the world practices like that.
She looks straight ahead, walks mindfully.

Buddha Kanakamuni has taught:
Someone who masters her mind,
walking steadily on the holy path,
has nothing to worry about,
since she dwells in mindfulness.

Buddha Kashyapa has taught:
Someone who does not cause others to suffer,
who is diligent in doing goodness,
purifies her mind.
This is what the Buddha teaches.

Buddha Shakyamuni has taught:
By guarding our actions of body and speech,
we purify our minds.
If you are able to do this,
you realize your nature of no-birth and no-death. [Bell]

Sharing the Merit

Venerable Bhikshunis, please join your palms so that we can offer up the merit of our recitation together.

To respect and put into practice
the wonderful Pratimoksha,
to leave behind the world of birth and death
and be able to realize nirvana,
is to realize the highest happiness.

For as long as the precepts endure,
the teachings of the Buddha endure.
To recite and protect the precepts
means that the Buddha is always present,
forever in the world. [Bell]

Reciting the Vinaya
practicing the way of awareness,
gives rise to benefits without limit.
We vow to share the fruits with all beings.
We vow to offer tribute to parents, teachers, friends, and numerous
    beings
who give guidance and support along the path.
[Bell] [Bell] [Bell]

Sangha Restoration Offenses:
Methods for Practicing Dwelling Apart, Beginning Anew, and Purifying the Offense

IF A BHIKSHU or bhikshuni transgresses a Sangha Restoration Offense and admits the offense on the same day, he or she only needs to practice six days of Beginning Anew. After that, the offense can be formally declared purified with a Sanghakarman Procedure. If he or she hides the offense, then after it is admitted, he or she has to practice Dwelling Apart (Manatva) for as many days as the offense was concealed. After that, she or he practices six days of Beginning Anew and then asks the Sangha to declare the offense purified. For example, if a bhikshu concealed his offense for forty days, he has to practice Dwelling Apart for forty days before he begins to practice six days of Beginning Anew. (Note: For bhikshunis there are fifteen days of Beginning Anew.)

During the time he or she practices Dwelling Apart, the monk or nun should live more simply than usual, deprived of certain comforts and should practice more manual work than normal, in order to be reminded that he or she is practicing Dwelling Apart. During this time, bhikshus and bhikshunis cannot receive the prostration of others, cannot have an attendant, cannot teach the Dharma, cannot attend Dharma Discussions, and cannot hold positions such as Guest Master, Work Coordinator and so on.

Text of Admitting a Sangha Restoration Offense

Noble Sangha, please listen to me: I am Bhikshu / Bhikshuni _____.
I have transgressed the precept _____. I have hidden the offense for
_____ days before admitting my offense. Now I admit my offense and
ask to receive a period of Dwelling Apart for _____ days before
practicing a further six / fifteen days of Beginning Anew. Venerable Bhikshus / Bhikshunis, please be compassionate and bear witness to my
request.

Text of an Announcement to Be Made Every Day while Practicing Dwelling Apart

Noble Sangha, please listen to me: I am Bhikshu / Bhikshuni _____.
I have transgressed the precept _____. I hid the offense for
_____ days before admitting my offense. The Sangha is allowing
me to practice a period of Dwelling Apart for _____ days before practicing six / fifteen days of Beginning Anew, and today I am practicing my
_____ th day and I have _____ more days to practice. I am fully aware
that I am practicing Dwelling Apart. Venerable Bhikshus / Bhikshunis,
please be compassionate and bear witness to my announcement.

Text to Request to Practice Six or Fifteen Days of Beginning Anew

Noble Sangha, please listen to me: I am Bhikshu / Bhikshuni _____.
I have transgressed the precept _____. I hid the offense for _____

days before admitting my offense. The Sangha allowed me to practice a period of Dwelling Apart for _____ days, and I have completed that period of practice. Now I request the Sangha to allow me to begin the practice of Beginning Anew for six/fifteen days. Venerable Bhikshus/Bhikshunis, please be compassionate and bear witness to my request.

Text of an Announcement To Be Made Every Day while Practicing Six or Fifteen Days of Beginning Anew

Noble Sangha, please listen to me: I am Bhikshu/Bhikshuni _____.
I have transgressed the precept _____. I hid the offense for _____ days before admitting my offense. The Sangha allowed me to practice a period of Dwelling Apart for _____ days, and I have completed that period of Dwelling Apart. I have also been allowed to practice six/fifteen days of Beginning Anew, and today I am practicing my _____th day and I have _____ more days to practice. I am fully aware that I am practicing six/fifteen days of Beginning Anew before the formal purification of my offense. Venerable Bhikshus/Bhikshunis, please be compassionate and bear witness to my announcement.

Text for Requesting Purification of a Sangha Restoration Offense

Noble Sangha, please listen to me: I am Bhikshu/Bhikshuni _____.
I have transgressed the precept _____. I hid the offense for _____ days before admitting my offense. The Sangha allowed me to practice a period of Dwelling Apart for _____ days, and I have completed that

period of practice and six/fifteen days of Beginning Anew. Venerable Bhikshus/Bhikshunis, now I am requesting you to formally purify my offense. Please be compassionate and bear witness to my request.

Release and Expression of Regret Offenses:
Methods for Practicing Expressing Regret and Beginning Anew to be made before the whole Sangha or before three or two bhikshus representing the whole Sangha

THE BHIKSHU/BHIKSHUNI presents the object or money that he or she wishes to release and hands it to the Sangha, and says: Noble Sangha, please listen to me. I am Bhikshu/Bhikshuni _____. I transgressed the precepts in holding and using this object, money or possession. Now I wish to release it and hand it over to the Sangha.

The bhikshu/bhikshuni hands the object or money to a bhikshu/bhikshuni who is representing the Sangha and says: Noble Sangha, please listen to me. I am Bhikshu/Bhikshuni _____. I transgressed the precepts in holding and using this object, money or possession. Now I have released it and handed it over to the Sangha so that the Sangha can do with it whatever they see fit or, if necessary, destroy it. I wish to admit my transgression and express my regret. I promise I shall not do this again. Venerable Bhikshus/Bhikshunis, please be compassionate and bear witness to this expression of my regret.

The bhikshu/bhikshuni who is representing the Sangha says: Bhik-shu/Bhikshuni _____, you have been able to admit your offense, express your regret, and begin anew. Your precepts' body is again clear.

Conclusion: Step by Step

THE GOAL of the Revised Pratimoksha is to respond to the current needs of the Sangha and protect the individual monks and nuns. This does not mean to say that it cannot be improved in the future. In fact, it is only by doing exactly this that we will be practicing according to the spirit of the Buddha, for the Buddha himself improved many precepts.

Let us look at the precept not to kill. At first this precept prohibited monastics from killing people, but when some monks killed themselves, the precept was revised. These unfortunate monks heard the Buddha's teachings on the impurity and impermanence of the body, and they began to feel tired of life. Therefore they said very negative and pessimistic things like "What is the point of living? I might as well kill myself." Responding to this situation, the Buddha added that if we encourage people to kill themselves, if we praise killing, if we have the idea that it is good to kill, then we are also breaking the precept. In other cases, sometimes the Buddha would eliminate a precept altogether if it no longer had a role to play. This is why it is important to allow the precepts to ripen over time, improving them constantly. We have to make them really serve the Sangha. Every ten or twenty years, they need to be revised. We should not be too proud and think that this Revised Pratimoksha is perfect. It still has weaknesses.

In the future, people might say: "This precept was made by my teacher and by my elders so you cannot change it." But this is going in the opposite direction from what your teacher wants, from what the high monks and nuns who made these precepts want. You have to continue this work and improve the precepts so that they are more applicable to the time and place in which you are living.

Three Dimensions of the Precepts

In addition to ensuring that each precept is applicable and appropriate to the situation, is of benefit, and protects the Sangha and the individual, there are three dimensions which we should also look for in each precept. Each dimension adds depth and breadth to our practice of the precepts. These are three containers for keeping our precepts' body pure. They can be called the three accumulations for purifying the practice of the precepts because with each dimension we accumulate more purity in our practice of the precepts.

The first dimension is refraining from negative action. This is called *samvara sila* in Sanskrit. "Samvara" means to keep, not to break and "sila" means precepts. Refraining means we are determined not to do something. We stop. When we refrain from doing a negative action, we conserve something. You hold your alms bowl so that it does not fall down and break. You also hold your precepts like that. You keep your precepts so that they are intact, they are not broken. The monk on the Yen Tu Mountain who became a master of the Bamboo Forest school in the 13th century wrote a poem about holding the precepts so that they do not fall.

Master Guishan says that refraining is to keep or hold the precepts, whereas to perform negative action is to break the precepts. We should not do something even if we feel pushed to do it. We have to hold ourselves, to prevent ourselves from doing this negative action. Action here refers to the three actions of body, speech, and mind: in other words, physical actions, speech, and thoughts.

The second dimension is performing, doing positive action. This is called *kushaladharma sila*. "Kushala" means good in Sanskrit, "dharma" means things. An example is the precepts' recitation. If we refrain from reciting the precepts, we would break the precepts. Or if we did not attend the three-month rains' retreat each year, we would break the precepts. In the case of positive or wholesome action, refraining leads to breaking and performing leads to holding or keeping.

If you see someone fall down and hurt himself and you do nothing, you break the precepts. If a person needs us and may fall into a difficult situation without our help, we break the precepts if we don't reach out to help that person.

If we have the opportunity to rescue an animal and we do not do it, then we break the precepts. If we see anyone being abused and we just sit there in meditation, not taking any notice, we break the precepts. We may think, "It is not my business, why should I tire myself intervening?" We have to intervene in these cases in order to stop what is going on. For example, in a situation of war, where there is invasion, oppression, and injustice, we have to ask "What can I do, what can I say to increase awareness about this situation of oppression and suffering?" We should make people aware that they can come together to stop the war. If we just say: "Go ahead and fight if you want to fight. Life and death is up to you," that would not be keeping the precept; that is not wholesome practice.

We have to do what is needed to be done. We see someone dying of hunger, but we hesitate; we see someone drowning and we hesitate, saying, "Oh, it's cold." We have to jump down and help that person. We have to find a way to offer that hungry person food. There is a law now in France that if you are sitting on the bus or the subway and you see someone beating or killing another person and you do nothing, then you are breaking the law. When you see something happening that should not be happening, something unjust, then you have to intervene. Non-intervention is refraining when you should take action. In some countries we are legally required to seek help when we see others suffer. How much more so, as practitioners, should we reach out to help and prevent danger and suffering to others around us.

The third dimension is doing something to benefit living beings. It is called *sattvarthakriya sila*. "Sattva" means living beings and "arth" means to benefit. "Kriya" means group, collection or set. If nothing negative is happening in the present moment, it is not necessary to intervene to help. Yet we must still have the heart of compassion. Perhaps we know that in this present moment there is no urgent situation in which we need to intervene to put an end to suffering. But still, we are aware that in the world there are so many living beings imprisoned and suffering - in Iraq, in the Middle East, in Africa, or right in our own community or city. There are children dying of hunger who have had nothing to eat for days. Sitting here, our compassion wakes us up. Simply enjoying our peaceful situation, we do not feel happy; we do not feel at ease. We want to do something to alleviate the suffering in the world. There is not an urgent need immediately around us, but we know that there are situations in the world that need our help. We can reach out our hands very far to help. We have to do something good, not because if we don't do it we will be put in prison, but because we really want to do it. We have a good heart and we want to help.

This is the spirit of the Vinaya. In it there is the way of the bodhisattva, the awakened person who is animated by compassion. If we think that the precepts are only there to tell us what we should not do, our perspective is not large enough. In all the precepts for both novices and fully ordained monastics, there is a lot of mention of refraining from doing particular acts. If we look deeper into the precepts, we see that they could be more positive. Telling us not to do things is only one part of the precepts. The bodhisattva ideal to help others means that the precepts must have another aspect. Not killing is good already, but it is not enough — you also have to protect life, you have to make life beautiful and worth living. To fully practice the precepts you have to practice refraining from unwholesome action, performing wholesome action, and making the world better for all living beings.

These three dimensions allow us to fully embrace the Vinaya. Within each dimension we can identify the other two dimensions. We do not kill and at the same moment we are protecting life. We protect life and at the same time we are protecting and supporting future generations, we are nourishing the heart and mind of love in ourselves and in others. The three dimensions inter-are with each other. We should continue to integrate these three dimensions into the precepts so that those who study and practice the precepts can touch these dimensions, and our practice of the precepts can remain fresh and alive.

In bringing the Pratimoksha up to date we have to go step by step. The first step has been to revise the precepts as we have done, making them relevant and applicable to modern life. The next step is to bring in these three dimensions.

The Revised Pratimoksha still carries the spirit of refraining from negative action more than the other two dimensions. We cannot see so clearly the aspects of performing wholesome action and benefiting living beings. After ten or twenty years, the international body of bhikshus and bhikshunis have to make a further revision so that each precept has these three aspects. The Pratimoksha needs to be continuously revised so that it will be applicable, inspiring, and appropriate for the practice of fully ordained monks and nuns. If we do this, we are being kind to the Buddha; we are being the Buddha's true continuation.

Parallax Press publishes books on engaged Buddhism and the practice of mind-fulness by Thich Nhat Hanh and other authors. As a division of the Unified Buddhist Church, we are committed to making these teachings accessible to everyone and preserving them for future generations. We believe that, in doing so, we help alleviate suffering and create a more peaceful world. All of Thich Nhat Hanh's work is available at our on-line store and in our free catalog. For a copy of the catalog, please contact:

Parallax Press
P.O. Box 7355
Berkeley, CA 94707
www.parallax.org
Tel: (510) 525-0101

Monastics and laypeople practice the art of mindful living in the tradition of Thich Nhat Hanh at retreat communities in France and the United States. Individuals, couples, and families are invited to join these communities for a Day of Mindfulness and longer practice periods. For information, please visit www.plumvillage.org or contact:

Plum Village
13 Martineau
33580 Dieulivol, France
info@plumvillage.org

Green Mountain Dharma Center
P.O. Box 182
Hartland Four Corners, VT 05049
mfmaster@vermontel.net
Tel: (802) 436-1103

Deer Park Monastery
2499 Melru Lane
Escondido, CA 92026
deerpark@plumvillage.org
Tel: (760) 291-1003

For a worldwide directory of Sanghas practicing in the tradition of Thich Nhat Hanh, please visit www.iamhome.org.